Daily Devotional for Women

1 YEAR, 5-MINUTE DAILY DEVOTIONAL FOR CHRISTIAN WOMEN

ANCHORED GRACE PUBLISHING

A Gift for You

Thank you for choosing this devotional.

To support your journey of faith, we created a special gift bundle for our readers.

Inside the Anchored Grace Reader Gift Bundle, you will receive:

A free digital devotional

Printable prayer journal pages

Scripture reflection cards

Bonus devotionals for different seasons of life

Daily encouragement from Anchored Grace

Simply scan the QR code below or visit the link to receive your free bundle.

devo.anchoredgraces.com/2026gift

Scan the QR code with your phone camera or type the link into your browser.

We pray these resources continue to encourage your heart each day.

January 1

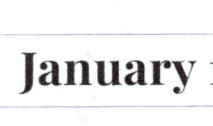

New Beginnings with God

"See, I am doing a new thing! Now it springs up; do you not perceive it? I am making a way in the wilderness and streams in the wasteland."
Isaiah 43:19

DEVOTIONAL

In every new season of life, God invites us to cultivate our hopes and dreams, even when it feels daunting.

DAILY REFLECTION

What new beginnings is God inviting you to embrace in this season of your life? How can you open your heart to His leading?

PRAYER

Dear God, thank you for the gift of new beginnings. Help me to trust in Your plans and to embrace the changes ahead with faith and courage.

Every ending is merely a new beginning wrapped in grace.

January 2

Trusting God's Timing

"Trust in the Lord with all your heart and lean not on your own understanding." **Proverbs 3:5-6**

DEVOTIONAL

In this season of your life, remember that every moment is an opportunity to deepen your trust in God's plan; His timing will lead you to places you never thought you'd go.

DAILY REFLECTION

What areas of your life do you find yourself struggling to trust God's timing? How might surrendering these concerns to Him change your perspective?

PRAYER

Dear Lord, help me to embrace your perfect timing in my life. Remind me that your plans for me are good, allowing me to find peace and trust in each moment.

Patience is not just waiting: it's a chance to grow in grace.

January 3

Embracing Grace, Not Perfection

"Consider how the wildflowers grow. They do not labor or spin. Yet I tell you, not even Solomon in all his splendor was dressed like one of these. If that is how God clothes the grass of the field, how much more will he clothe you, you of little faith?" **Luke 12:27-28**

DEVOTIONAL

As you embrace your unique journey, remember that grace invites you to let go of perfection and find peace in the beautiful chaos of life.

DAILY REFLECTION

What would it look like in your life to embrace grace rather than striving for unattainable perfection? How might your days change if you offered yourself the same kindness and understanding you give to others?

PRAYER

Dear God, help me to let go of my need for perfection and to embrace the beautiful messiness of life. Remind me to see Your grace in every moment and to extend it to myself as I navigate the challenges of motherhood and beyond.

Grace fills the gaps where perfection fails.

January 4

Finding Peace in God's Presence

"My soul finds rest in God alone; my salvation comes from him. Truly he is my rock and my salvation; he is my fortress, I will never be shaken."
Psalm 62:1-2

DEVOTIONAL

Remember, dear one, in the busyness of daily life, finding peace begins by cultivating intentional moments in God's presence where you can truly be yourself and experience His loving embrace.

DAILY REFLECTION

What does it mean for you to find peace in God's presence today? Can you identify a moment when you felt His calming influence in your life? Take a moment to consider how you can invite that presence into your everyday routine.

PRAYER

Dear Lord, I come before You seeking the peace that only You can provide. Help me to pause, breathe, and embrace Your presence in every moment of my day. Amen.

In His presence, worries dissolve, and peace finds a home.

January 5

Your Identity in Christ

"Therefore, if anyone is in Christ, the new creation has come: The old has gone, the new is here!" **2 Corinthians 5:17**

DEVOTIONAL

You are defined by God's love and purpose, not the myriad of roles you fulfill; lean into your true identity in Christ.

DAILY REFLECTION

What does being rooted in Christ mean to you, especially during the busy seasons of motherhood and life? How can you embrace your true identity in Him today?

PRAYER

Heavenly Father, thank you for reminding me of who I am in You. Help me to embrace my identity as Your beloved daughter today, filling my heart with confidence and grace.

Your worth is not defined by your to-do list,
but by the unchanging love of Christ.

January 6

God's Faithfulness Through the Years

"The steadfast love of the Lord never ceases; his mercies never come to an end; they are new every morning." **Lamentations 3:22-23**

DEVOTIONAL

God's faithfulness manifests in the little moments, affirming that your journey, with all its twists and turns, is part of His beautiful plan for you and your family.

DAILY REFLECTION

What moments in your life can you look back on and recognize God's faithfulness, even when things felt uncertain or challenging?

PRAYER

Dear God, thank you for the steady presence you have been in our lives. Help me to embrace your faithfulness each day, trusting in your plan as I navigate this journey of motherhood and life.

In every season, God's faithfulness shines brighter
as we learn to trust and lean upon Him.

January 7

Strength for the Journey

"She is clothed with strength and dignity; she can laugh at the days to come." **Proverbs 31:25**

DEVOTIONAL

Strength for our journey often comes from acknowledging both our struggles and our joys, making us resilient and beautifully imperfect.

DAILY REFLECTION

What are the challenges you're currently facing, and how can you invite God's strength into your journey today?

PRAYER

Dear God, thank You for being our source of strength. As I navigate the challenges of motherhood and life, fill me with Your peace and guide my steps with Your unwavering support.

Your strength is not just about enduring;
it's about embracing the journey with grace and hope.

January 8

A Quiet Heart in a Noisy World

"In repentance and rest is your salvation, in quietness and trust is your strength." **Isaiah 30:15**

DEVOTIONAL

In the whirlwind of motherhood and daily responsibilities, remember to carve out moments of quiet for your soul, finding strength and peace amidst the noise.

DAILY REFLECTION

What are the noisy distractions in your life that keep you from experiencing the peace and stillness you crave? How might you set aside time today to cultivate a quieter heart amidst the busyness of motherhood and daily responsibilities?

PRAYER

Dear Lord, help me find moments of stillness in the chaos. Grant me a quiet heart that rests in Your presence, and let me be mindful of Your peace in my everyday life.

Peace is not the absence of noise,
but the presence of Christ in our hearts.

One Week Together

You've just completed your first week of devotionals.

If these reflections have brought peace or encouragement into your day, would you consider sharing a short Amazon review?

devo.anchoredgraces.com/2026

Your words help other women discover devotionals that may support them on their own faith journey.

Thank you for spending these moments in reflection.

January 9

Courage to Let Go

"Forget the former things; do not dwell on the past. See, I am doing a new thing! Now it springs up; do you not perceive it?" **Isaiah 43:18-19**

DEVOTIONAL

Letting go can be a profound act of courage that opens you to the joys and opportunities awaiting you in this new season of life.

DAILY REFLECTION

What are the things in your life that you hold onto tightly, and how might offering them to God bring you peace and new opportunities?

PRAYER

Dear Lord, help me to find the courage to release what no longer serves me. Teach me to trust in Your plan and embrace the freedom that comes from letting go.

Letting go is not losing: it's making space for what truly matters.

January 10

When You Feel Overlooked

"Since you are precious and honored in my sight, and because I love you, I will give people in exchange for you, nations in exchange for your life."
Isaiah 43:4

DEVOTIONAL

You are not defined by the recognition of others; your value is inherent and seen by those who truly matter in your life.

DAILY REFLECTION

What moments in your life have you felt overlooked, and how can you invite God into those feelings today?

PRAYER

Dear Lord, help me to recognize my worth in Your eyes and to remember that I am never unseen by You. Fill my heart with peace as I navigate feelings of being overlooked and remind me of the love you have for me.

Even in the quiet moments,
You are writing my story with love and purpose.

January 11

Resting in His Promises

"Fear not, for I am with you; be not dismayed, for I am your God; I will strengthen you, I will help you, I will uphold you with my righteous right hand." **Isaiah 41:10**

DEVOTIONAL

When life becomes overwhelming, remember to lean into God's promises, finding peace and strength in His faithful presence.

DAILY REFLECTION

What promises from God do you find yourself clinging to during your busiest days, and how do they bring you a sense of peace?

PRAYER

Dear Lord, help me to slow down and lean into Your promises. May I find comfort and strength in Your words as I navigate the demands of my daily life. Thank You for being my refuge and my guide.

Resting in His promises is not a sign of weakness, but an acknowledgment of His strength.

January 12

Beauty from Brokenness

"He heals the brokenhearted and binds up their wounds."
Psalm 147:3

DEVOTIONAL

You are a testament to the beauty that can emerge from life's challenges, reminding you that every scar carries a lesson of resilience and grace.

DAILY REFLECTION

What broken pieces in your life have you seen transformed into something beautiful? How can you embrace those moments as part of your journey?

PRAYER

Dear God, thank you for your unwavering love and the beauty you bring into our lives, even in our brokenness. Help us to see and celebrate the unique stories that shape us, trusting that you can make all things new.

In every scar lies a story of resilience and grace.

January 13

The Power of Prayer

"Do not be anxious about anything, but in every situation, by prayer and petition, with thanksgiving, present your requests to God. 7 And the peace of God, which transcends all understanding, will guard your hearts and your minds in Christ Jesus." **Philippians 4:6-7**

DEVOTIONAL

In the midst of life's busyness, remember that prayer is not just a ritual but a lifeline that connects you to divine guidance and peace.

DAILY REFLECTION

What are the prayers you whisper in the quiet moments of your day, and how do you feel God's presence within those sacred exchanges?

PRAYER

Dear Lord, thank you for the gift of prayer, a lifeline to connect with You amid life's busyness. Help me to remember that in every moment of chaos, I can find peace in Your presence.

Prayer is not just about asking:
it's about listening to the whisper of God in your heart.

January 14

Joy in the Ordinary

"Rejoice in the Lord always. I will say it again: Rejoice!"
Philippians 4:4

DEVOTIONAL

Joy often hides in the places we least expect; it's found in the laughter shared over breakfast, the quiet moments at bedtime, and the simple act of sharing your day.

DAILY REFLECTION

What mundane moments in your daily life bring you unexpected joy, and how can you savor them more deeply?

PRAYER

Dear God, thank you for the simple moments that often go unnoticed. Help me to find joy in the ordinary and to celebrate the gifts of each day.

Joy often hides in the most ordinary tasks, waiting to be discovered.

January 15

God's Wisdom for Today

"For the Lord gives wisdom; from his mouth come knowledge and understanding. He holds success in store for the upright, he is a shield to those whose walk is blameless..." **Proverbs 2:6-7**

DEVOTIONAL

God's wisdom today reminds us that within the chaos of life, there lies a gentle nudging toward our true purpose, urging us to seek understanding in our hearts rather than validation from the world.

DAILY REFLECTION

What is one area of your life where you feel you need God's wisdom the most right now? How might you open your heart to receive His guidance?

PRAYER

Dear God, thank you for the gift of Your wisdom that is ever-present in our lives. Help me to seek You with an open heart today and trust in Your plans for me and my family.

True wisdom comes not from our own understanding but from leaning into God's heart.

January 16

Freedom from Fear

"Do not be afraid of sudden fear, nor of the onslaught of the wicked when it comes; for the Lord will be your confidence and will keep your foot from."
Proverbs 3:25-26

DEVOTIONAL

The freedom from fear begins when we embrace our vulnerabilities and allow others to walk alongside us on this path of motherhood and life.

DAILY REFLECTION

What fears are you holding onto that might be keeping you from experiencing the fullness of life God has for you? How might surrendering these fears open the door to new beginnings and greater joy?

PRAYER

Dear Lord, thank You for being our refuge and strength. Help me to trust in You and find freedom from the fears that weigh me down. Grant me peace as I lean into Your guidance every day.

Freedom from fear begins when we choose to trust in God's faithfulness.

January 17

A Heart Anchored in Hope

"Why, my soul, are you downcast? Why so disturbed within me? Put your hope in God, for I will yet praise him, my Savior and my God." **Psalm 42:11**

DEVOTIONAL

In your journey as a mother and woman, remember that even on difficult days, your spirit can be renewed by reflecting on the blessings and resilience God has instilled in you.

DAILY REFLECTION

What anchors your heart in hope during life's challenging moments, and how can you cultivate that sense of hope daily?

PRAYER

Lord, thank You for being our steady anchor. Help us to find peace in Your promises and to nurture a heart filled with hope in all circumstances.

Hope is not the absence of storms,
but the quiet assurance that our anchor holds firm.

January 18

Living with Eternal Purpose

"But our citizenship is in heaven, and we eagerly await a Savior from there, the Lord Jesus Christ." **Philippians 3:20**

DEVOTIONAL

Life's greatest fulfillment arises when we align our daily actions with our God-given purpose, recognizing that even the smallest moments can carry eternal significance.

DAILY REFLECTION

What does living with eternal purpose look like in your daily life? How can you align your moments, big and small, with the deeper meaning God has placed in your heart?

PRAYER

Dear God, help me to embrace each day with a sense of purpose rooted in You. May my actions and decisions reflect Your love and light, as I navigate the beautiful complexities of motherhood and life.

Every moment is an opportunity to sew seeds of eternal significance.

January 19

Trusting God with Family

"They will have no fear of bad news; their hearts are steadfast, trusting in the Lord." **Psalm 112:7**

DEVOTIONAL

Trusting God with family means letting go of our need to control and embracing the journey with faith.

DAILY REFLECTION

What are the areas in your family life where you struggle to fully trust God, and how might surrendering these concerns change your perspective?

PRAYER

Dear God, thank you for the gift of family and the joy and challenges that come with it. Help me to trust you more fully, knowing that you have a purpose in every situation.

Trusting God with my family means letting go of worry and holding on to faith.

January 20

When You Need Strength

"...but those who hope in the Lord will renew their strength. They will soar on wings like eagles; they will run and not grow weary, they will walk and not be faint." **Isaiah 40:31**

DEVOTIONAL

When you feel overwhelmed, remember that true strength comes from leaning on your faith, enabling you to rise above life's demands with grace.

DAILY REFLECTION

What are the challenges you're facing right now that are making you feel weak, and how can you invite God into those moments for renewed strength?

PRAYER

Dear God, I come before You today with a heart seeking strength. Fill me with Your peace and empower me to face each day with courage and hope.

Strength is not the absence of struggle. but the presence of a God who carries us through.

January 21

Listening for God's Whisper

*"And your ears shall hear a word behind you, saying, 'This is the way, walk in it,' whenever you turn to the right or to the left." **Isaiah 30:21***

DEVOTIONAL

In the still moments of your day, remember that cultivating space for God's whispers can lead you toward renewed purpose and serenity.

DAILY REFLECTION

What distractions in your life might be keeping you from truly hearing God's whisper? How can you create moments of quiet to listen more closely?

PRAYER

Dear God, help me to quiet my heart and mind so that I can hear Your gentle whispers. Guide me in moments of stillness, and open my ears to Your loving voice.

In the stillness, God's whispers become clearer, leading us gently along the path of life.

January 22

Becoming a Woman of the Word

"Your word is a lamp for my feet, a light on my path."
Psalm 119:105

DEVOTIONAL

Let the Word of God be your guide and source of strength, reminding you that it's not just about being a parent or a professional; it's about nurturing your spirit and wisdom for all the roles you carry.

DAILY REFLECTION

What are the ways you can immerse yourself in God's Word this week, and how can it shape your thoughts and actions as a mother and woman of faith?

PRAYER

Dear Lord, thank you for the gift of Your Word. Help me to dive deeper into its truths and allow those truths to envelop my heart and guide my life. Amen.

Becoming a woman of the Word is not just about reading; it's about living the love and wisdom found on its pages.

Three Weeks of Reflection

You've now spent several weeks walking through these devotionals.

If this book has encouraged your heart, a brief Amazon review helps other women find the same encouragement.

devo.anchoredgraces.com/2026

Your experience may guide someone else toward the hope they are searching for.

Thank you for being here.

January 23

Healing Through Scripture

"Bless the Lord, O my soul, and forget not all his benefits, who forgives all your iniquity, who heals all your diseases." **Psalm 103:2-3**

DEVOTIONAL

In moments of weariness, revisit the scriptures, for within them lies the healing balm your spirit longs for.

DAILY REFLECTION

What is a scripture that brings you peace or comfort during difficult times, and how can you lean into that verse this week as you seek healing?

PRAYER

Dear Lord, as I turn to Your Word, help me to find solace and strength in your promises. May Your healing touch renew my spirit and fill my heart with hope and joy.

Scripture is not just words on a page;
it is the balm that soothes the soul and ignites the spirit.

January 24

When Life Feels Heavy

"Cast your burden on the Lord, and He will sustain you; He will never permit the righteous to be moved." **Psalm 55:22**

DEVOTIONAL

In those heavy moments, remember that it's okay to release your burdens and lean into the support that surrounds you.

DAILY REFLECTION

What burdens are you carrying today that feel too heavy to bear alone?

PRAYER

Dear God, please lighten my heart today and remind me of Your strength in my weakness. Help me to cast my cares on You and trust in Your endless love.

In the heaviest of moments, remember that you are never alone;
God walks beside you.

January 25

God's Grace for Past Mistakes

"Therefore, there is now no condemnation for those who are in Christ Jesus." **Romans 8:1**

DEVOTIONAL

Your past does not define your worth; God's grace is always available to lift you from the shadows of regret into the light of hope.

DAILY REFLECTION

What past mistakes linger in your heart that you need to release to God's grace today? How might embracing His forgiveness change the way you move forward in your life?

PRAYER

Dear Lord, thank You for Your endless grace and mercy. Help me to let go of my past and embrace the beauty of new beginnings. Fill my heart with Your peace and guidance as I continue this journey.

God's grace transforms our scars into stories of hope.

January 26

Living Loved

"Beloved, let us love one another, for love is from God; and whoever loves has been born of God and knows God." **1 John 4:7**

DEVOTIONAL

Embrace the love that surrounds you, for it empowers you to be the nurturing woman you were created to be.

DAILY REFLECTION

What does it mean for you to truly live loved in your daily life, as a mother and a woman? How can you open your heart to embrace the love that surrounds you?

PRAYER

Dear Lord, help me to see and embrace the love You have for me in every moment. May I live boldly and freely, filled with the knowledge that I am cherished, just as I am.

Living loved means allowing the warmth of grace to permeate your thoughts and actions.

January 27

Decluttering the Soul

"Create in me a clean heart, O God, and renew a right spirit within me."
Psalm 51:10

DEVOTIONAL

Sometimes, decluttering our physical space can lead to profound emotional and spiritual renewal, reminding us that it's alright to let go of the old to make way for the new.

DAILY REFLECTION

What old thoughts or emotional burdens are you holding onto that no longer serve your spirit?

PRAYER

Dear Lord, help me to recognize what's cluttering my heart and mind. Cleanse my spirit and guide me as I let go of the unnecessary, making space for Your love and peace.

Just as a physical space can become cluttered, so too can our souls; it's time to clear out what no longer nurtures us.

January 28

Rooted and Grounded in Love

"that Christ may dwell in your hearts through faith, and that you, being rooted and grounded in love, may have strength to comprehend with all the saints what is the breadth and length and height and depth of love."
Ephesians 3:17-19

DEVOTIONAL

Remember that when you root yourself in the nourishing love of God, you grow in strength and grace, allowing you to share that love abundantly with those around you.

DAILY REFLECTION

What does it mean for you to feel rooted and grounded in love amidst the busyness of motherhood and daily life? How can you cultivate that sense of stability and connection in your relationships?

PRAYER

Dear God, thank You for the gift of love that surrounds me. Help me to root myself deeper in Your love so I can reflect that same love to my family and others around me. Amen.

Love is not just a sentiment; it's the foundation that holds us steady in the storms of life.

January 29

Guarding Your Heart

"Above all else, guard your heart, for everything you do flows from it."
Proverbs 4:23

DEVOTIONAL

The heart is a precious treasure; guard it with intention, nurturing what brings you joy and releasing what holds you back.

DAILY REFLECTION

What are the specific areas of your life where you need to be more intentional about guarding your heart against negativity or hurtful influences? Reflect on how you can cultivate a more positive and nurturing environment for yourself and your loved ones.

PRAYER

Dear Lord, help me to guard my heart with wisdom and grace. May I find strength in Your love, shielding me from hurt and negativity as I navigate my role as a mom, friend, and woman of faith.

Your heart is a precious treasure;
guard it well to nurture the love it holds.

January 30

A Faith That Endures

"I can do all things through Christ who strengthens me."
Philippians 4:13

DEVOTIONAL

In your journey through the complexities of motherhood and life, remember that enduring faith is built on the foundation of remembering God's past faithfulness in your life.

DAILY REFLECTION

What does it mean to you to have a faith that stands firm through life's challenges? How have you experienced God's presence in your moments of struggle?

PRAYER

Dear God, thank You for being a constant source of strength in our lives. Help us to lean into our faith during times of uncertainty, knowing that You are always with us. Amen.

Enduring faith is not the absence of doubt,
but the assurance that we are never alone.

January 31

Stepping into the New with Boldness

"The Lord is my light and my salvation; whom shall I fear? The Lord is the stronghold of my life; of whom shall I be afraid?" **Psalm 27:1**

DEVOTIONAL

Stepping into the new can be daunting, but embracing change with boldness can lead to the rediscovery of passions and purposes long forgotten.

DAILY REFLECTION

What new opportunities or challenges is God inviting you to embrace with courage in this season of your life? How can you step forward in faith, trusting that He will guide you?

PRAYER

Dear Lord, thank You for the gift of new beginnings and opportunities. Help me to embrace the changes before me with confidence and trust in Your plan for my life. Amen.

Bravery is not the absence of fear, but the courage to move forward despite it.

February 1

Choosing Faith Over Feelings

"So faith comes from hearing, and hearing through the word of Christ."
Romans 10:17

DEVOTIONAL

Trusting God means choosing to believe in His promises over our ever-changing emotions, reminding us that His strength carries us through each challenging moment.

DAILY REFLECTION

What feelings have been pulling you away from faith lately? How can you intentionally choose to focus on God's promises instead?

PRAYER

Dear God, as I navigate the ups and downs of life, help me to anchor my heart in Your truth rather than my fleeting feelings. Grant me the courage to choose faith when doubts arise and remind me of Your unwavering love.

Faith isn't about feeling strong; it's about trusting that God's strength is enough.

February 2

The God Who Sees You

"You are the God who sees me."
Genesis 16:13

DEVOTIONAL

The take-home message here is that God recognizes the unseen struggles of our hearts and reassures us that we are never truly invisible to Him.

DAILY REFLECTION

What moments in your life have made you feel invisible or overlooked? How can you lean into the truth that God sees you, even in the mundane or challenging seasons of motherhood? Reflect on how this understanding can reshape your perspective today.

PRAYER

Dear God, thank You for being present in our lives and for seeing us even when we feel unseen. Help us to grasp the depth of Your love and awareness in our daily struggles and joys.

You are loved and seen by the One who knows you inside and out.

February 3

Loving Others from a Full Heart

"And walk in love, as Christ loved us and gave himself up for us, a fragrant offering and sacrifice to God." **Ephesians 5:2**

DEVOTIONAL

Loving others becomes a joyful act when we nurture our own hearts and spirits first.

DAILY REFLECTION

What does it look like for you to love others from a full heart, and how can gratitude deepen that love in your daily life?

PRAYER

Dear Lord, fill my heart with Your love so that I may overflow with kindness and compassion towards those around me. Help me to see others as You see them, reflecting Your grace in every interaction.

Love others not just from your abundance,
but from the wells of gratitude you cultivate within.

February 4

Waiting Well with God

"Wait for the Lord; be strong and take heart and wait for the Lord."
Psalm 27:14

DEVOTIONAL

God invites us to experience His presence even in our waiting, teaching us that the journey can be just as profound as the destination.

DAILY REFLECTION

What does waiting on God look like for you in this season of your life, and how can you embrace that waiting with hope and trust?

PRAYER

Dear God, thank you for being with me in every season. Help me to find joy and purpose as I wait on You, trusting that Your timing is perfect.

Waiting is not a time of inactivity,
but an opportunity to deepen our relationship with God.

February 5

Letting Go of Control

"For I know the plans I have for you," declares the Lord, "plans to prosper you and not to harm you, plans to give you hope and a future."
Jeremiah 29:11

DEVOTIONAL

Letting go of control frees us to experience the joy and beauty of life's unexpected moments.

DAILY REFLECTION

What does letting go of control look like in your daily life, and how can you embrace the beauty of uncertainty as you navigate motherhood and beyond?

PRAYER

Dear God, help me to release my grip on the things I cannot control. Grant me peace in knowing that You hold my life and my loved ones in Your hands. Thank You for guiding me as I learn to trust in Your plans.

Trusting in God's timing is the first step toward freedom from the burdens of control.

February 6

God's Mercy Is New Each Morning

"...weeping may endure for a night, but joy comes in the morning."
Psalm 30:5

DEVOTIONAL

God's mercy is a gentle reminder that every day is a chance to begin again, to forgive ourselves, and to embrace the promise of joy that awaits us.

DAILY REFLECTION

What burdens are weighing on your heart this morning, and how might remembering God's mercies help you release them?

PRAYER

Dear Lord, thank You for the gift of a new day filled with Your grace. Help me to embrace Your mercies, allowing them to refresh my spirit and guide my thoughts.

Every sunrise is a gentle reminder that God's love revitalizes us, no matter the mistakes of yesterday.

February 7

Walking in Confidence, Not Comparison

"Charm is deceptive, and beauty is fleeting; but a woman who fears the Lord is to be praised." **Proverbs 31:30**

DEVOTIONAL

Embrace the beauty of your own story and trust that your path is uniquely designed for you, free from the shadows of comparison.

DAILY REFLECTION

What areas of your life do you find yourself comparing to others, and how can embracing your unique journey lead to greater peace and confidence today?

PRAYER

Dear Lord, help me to see my worth through Your eyes. Let me focus on the gifts and strengths You have given me, and remind me that I am enough just as I am. Grant me the courage to celebrate others without diminishing my own accomplishments.

Your journey is uniquely crafted by God; comparing it to others only blurs the beautiful path meant uniquely for you.

February 8

When Prayers Go Unanswered

"Even to your old age and gray hairs I am he, I am he who will sustain you. I have made you and I will carry you; I will sustain you and I will rescue you." **Isaiah 46:4**

DEVOTIONAL

When prayers feel unanswered, remember that you are gently cradled in a love that sees the full tapestry of your journey.

DAILY REFLECTION

What is one prayer in your heart that feels unanswered, and how can you bring that before God today? How might this moment be an opportunity to deepen your trust in Him?

PRAYER

Dear Lord, in the silence of unanswered prayers, draw near to my heart and fill it with your peace. Help me to trust in your perfect timing and wisdom, knowing that you are always listening.

In the stillness of unanswered prayers,
God is crafting a deeper relationship with us.

February 9

Finding Joy in God Alone

"You make known to me the path of life; in your presence there is fullness of joy; at your right hand are pleasures forevermore." **Psalm 16:11**

DEVOTIONAL

True joy emerges from the intimate moments we share with God, reminding us that He is the ultimate source of fulfillment and peace, beyond our daily responsibilities.

DAILY REFLECTION

What are the moments in your daily life where you find it challenging to rest in the joy that comes from God alone? Reflect on how you can shift your focus to Him in those moments.

PRAYER

Dear Lord, thank You for being a constant source of joy in our lives. Help us to recognize and embrace Your presence in every situation we face today. Fill our hearts with Your peace and delight.

True joy is found not in the circumstances around us, but in the steadfast love of our God.

February 10

Your Life Still Has Purpose

"Many are the plans in a person's heart, but it is the Lord's purpose that prevails." **Proverbs 19:21**

DEVOTIONAL

No matter where you are in life's journey, remember that your experiences can guide and inspire others, giving your life renewed purpose.

DAILY REFLECTION

What passions and dreams have you set aside while tending to the responsibilities of motherhood and life? How might you reclaim them and explore new ways to embrace your purpose?

PRAYER

Dear God, thank You for the beautiful journey of life and the unique purpose You have for each of us. Help me to recognize and embrace the gifts I have, trusting in Your divine plan as I navigate this season of my life.

Your worth does not diminish with time; it only grows richer and more profound.

February 11

Speaking Life Over Yourself

"I praise you because I am fearfully and wonderfully made; your works are wonderful, I know that full well." **Psalm 139:14**

DEVOTIONAL

Embrace the truth that your words hold power, and make it a practice to speak life over yourself daily.

DAILY REFLECTION

What words do you speak over yourself when you face challenges and uncertainties in your life? How can you shift those words to speak life, affirmation, and grace into your own heart and soul?

PRAYER

Dear Lord, help me to see myself through Your loving eyes. May I choose to speak words of hope and encouragement over my life, embracing the beautiful truth of who I am in You.

Your words hold the power to shape your reality:
let them reflect the love and strength you carry within.

February 12

When You Feel Spiritually Dry

"When the poor and needy seek water, and there is none, and their tongue is parched with thirst, I, the Lord, will answer them; I, the God of Israel, will not forsake them." **Isaiah 41:17**

DEVOTIONAL

In the busyness of life, it's important to intentionally seek the refreshing presence of God, recognizing that He is ready to fill our hearts with living water.

DAILY REFLECTION

When was the last time you felt spiritually invigorated, and how can you invite that sense of renewal back into your life today?

PRAYER

Dear God, in this moment of weariness, fill my heart with your presence. Help me to seek you in the ordinary and find strength and joy in the journey of motherhood and faith.

Even in the desert, God's whispers can be heard
through the rustling leaves of hope.

February 13

Healed by His Word

"...humbly accept the word planted in you, which can save you."
James 1:21

DEVOTIONAL

The healing power of His Word is always within reach; we simply need to pause and listen.

DAILY REFLECTION

What is one negative thought or belief about yourself that God's Word can help you replace with truth?

PRAYER

Dear Lord, thank You for Your Word, which has the power to heal and transform our hearts. Help me to embrace Your promises and find comfort in Your truth today.

Healing begins when we allow His voice to drown out our doubts.

February 14

God's Love That Never Fails

"God is love, and whoever lives in love lives in God, and God in them."
1 John 4:16

DEVOTIONAL

In the midst of life's demands, take heart that God's love will never falter, empowering you to extend the same grace to yourself and your family.

DAILY REFLECTION

What does it mean to you, in your daily life, to experience a love that never fails, especially as a mom and caregiver? How can you reflect that unwavering love to those around you?

PRAYER

Dear God, thank you for your endless love that surrounds us each day. Help me to embrace your love and share it with my family and friends. May I always be a vessel of your grace and compassion.

God's love is the anchor that steadies our hearts amidst life's storms.

February 15

Overflowing with Gratitude

"Rejoice always, pray continually, give thanks in all circumstances; for this is God's will for you in Christ Jesus." **1 Thessalonians 5:16-18**

DEVOTIONAL

Life's beauty often lies in small, everyday moments; make it a practice to pause and give thanks, for gratitude transforms our perspective and enriches our souls.

DAILY REFLECTION

What small moment in your day can you choose to view through the lens of gratitude? How might that shift your perspective on the challenges you face?

PRAYER

Dear Lord, thank You for the many gifts You have poured into our lives. Help us to recognize and celebrate the blessings, big and small, that fill our days with joy and purpose.

Gratitude transforms what we have into enough, and more.

February 16

Forgiving Yourself and Others

"As far as the east is from the west, so far has he removed our transgressions from us." **Psalm 103:12**

DEVOTIONAL

No matter the scars of the past, forgiving ourselves and others opens the door to healing and deeper connections. Remember, as you navigate this journey, both receiving and offering forgiveness is an act of love that nurtures not only your spirit but also the hearts of those around you.

DAILY REFLECTION

What are the things you hold onto that keep you from fully embracing compassion for yourself and others? How might letting go of those burdens transform your relationships and inner peace?

PRAYER

Dear Lord, help me to extend grace to myself and those I encounter. As I navigate my journey, remind me that forgiveness is a path to healing and restoration.

Forgiveness is not just a gift we give to others;
it is the key that unlocks our own heart.

February 17

God's Strength in Your Weakness

"My grace is sufficient for you, for my power is made perfect in weakness."
2 Corinthians 12:9-10

DEVOTIONAL

In our toughest moments, rather than striving to uphold a facade of perfection, we can surrender our weaknesses to God, who is ready and willing to provide us with His boundless strength.

DAILY REFLECTION

What areas in your life do you feel weak or burdened, and how might you invite God into those feelings today?

PRAYER

Dear God, thank you for being my strength in times of struggle. Help me to feel your presence in my weaknesses and to trust in your power over my life.

In my weakness, He reveals His strength.

February 18

Anxious for Nothing

"...not worry about tomorrow, for tomorrow will worry about itself."
Matthew 6:34

DEVOTIONAL

In each moment of worry, there is an invitation to embrace the present and let go of what we cannot control.

DAILY REFLECTION

What worries or anxieties are you holding onto today, and how might you lay them down at Jesus' feet?

PRAYER

Dear God, as I navigate the worries of life, help me to trust in Your presence and peace. Remind me that I can release my fears into Your caring hands today.

Anxiety loses its power when surrendered to the One who holds our tomorrows.

February 19

Living a Legacy of Faith

"Let your light shine before others, that they may see your good deeds and glorify your Father in heaven." **Matthew 5:16**

DEVOTIONAL

The most impactful legacy is built through everyday moments of love and faith shared with those we cherish.

DAILY REFLECTION

What legacy of faith are you intentionally building for your family today, and how can you inspire those around you to continue that legacy in the years to come?

PRAYER

Dear God, thank You for the gift of family and the opportunity to share my faith. Help me to demonstrate Your love and grace in my daily life, so that I may pass down a meaningful legacy to my children and those around me.

Faith is not just a belief; it's a way of living that leaves footprints for others to follow.

February 20

Peace in the Midst of Change

"Be still, and know that I am God."
Psalm 46:10

DEVOTIONAL

In the midst of change, remember that God's peace is a constant, waiting for you to embrace it.

DAILY REFLECTION

What change are you currently facing in your life, and how can you invite God's peace into that situation?

PRAYER

Dear Lord, thank you for being a constant source of peace in our lives, even when everything around us feels uncertain. Help me to trust in Your plans and to lean on Your strength as I navigate through these changes.

True peace is not the absence of change but the presence of faith.

February 21

When You Feel Inadequate

"God is within her, she will not fall; God will help her at break of day."
Psalm 46:5

DEVOTIONAL

You are enough, just as you are, and your genuine love and care are what truly make a difference in your family's life.

DAILY REFLECTION

What are the moments in your life when you feel most inadequate, and how can you invite God into those feelings?

PRAYER

Dear God, please remind me that in my weakness, you are my strength. Help me embrace my imperfections and find peace in knowing I am enough because of your love.

In the tapestry of life, our imperfections are the threads that make us uniquely beautiful.

February 22

God Is Your Refuge

"I will say of the Lord, 'He is my refuge and my fortress, my God, in whom I trust.'" **Psalm 91:2**

DEVOTIONAL

Remember, dear one, that God is not just a destination for your burdens; He is your safe haven and steady stronghold amidst life's storms.

DAILY REFLECTION

What does it mean for you, in your daily life as a mother and woman, to find refuge in God amidst your challenges and responsibilities?

PRAYER

Dear Lord, thank You for being my safe haven and strength. Help me to lean on You when life feels overwhelming, and remind me that I am never alone in this journey.

Finding sanctuary in Him transforms the noise of our lives into a melody of peace.

February 23

Choosing Obedience Over Comfort

"For the moment all discipline seems painful rather than pleasant, but later it yields the peaceful fruit of righteousness to those who have been trained by it." **Hebrews 12:11**

DEVOTIONAL

Choosing to embrace obedience in the little nudges, even when it feels easier to retreat into comfort, opens the door to unexpected blessings and growth.

DAILY REFLECTION

What areas of your life is God calling you to step out of your comfort zone, and how can you lean into His guidance today?

PRAYER

Dear Lord, help me to embrace Your calling in my life, even when it feels challenging. Guide my steps as I choose obedience over comfort, trusting in Your perfect plan.

Obedience is not just a choice:
it's a pathway to deeper peace and purpose.

February 24

Be Still and Know

"Even there your hand will guide me; your right hand will hold me fast."
Psalm 139:10

DEVOTIONAL

When overwhelmed, take time to acknowledge that in the stillness, you can find clarity and strength for your journey ahead.

DAILY REFLECTION

What does it mean for you to be still in the midst of your busy life? How can you create moments of quiet to truly know and feel God's presence?

PRAYER

Dear God, help me to find peace in the chaos of my days. Grant me the wisdom to pause, reflect, and connect with You, even for just a moment. Thank You for Your constant presence in my life.

In the stillness, we discover the richness of God's love.

February 25

Pressing On When You're Weary

*"And let us not grow weary of doing good, for in due season we will reap, if we do not give up." **Galatians 6:9***

DEVOTIONAL

In those moments of weariness, remember that your perseverance is a testament to your love, and each small step forward is significant to your family's journey.

DAILY REFLECTION

What reminds you of God's strength in your life when you feel weary? How can you draw from that strength today?

PRAYER

Dear Lord, please fill my heart with Your peace and renew my energy. Help me to trust in Your provision and press on, even when I feel weary.

Even in our weariness, God's strength is a well that never runs dry.

February 26

God's Gentle Correction

*"My child, do not despise the Lord's discipline, and do not resent his rebuke, because the Lord disciplines those he loves, as a father the son he delights in." **Proverbs 3:11-12***

DEVOTIONAL

When God gently corrects us, it is an invitation to embrace simplicity and prioritize love in the chaos of life.

DAILY REFLECTION

What areas of your life is God gently prompting you to reevaluate, and how can you embrace His guidance with an open heart?

PRAYER

Dear Lord, thank you for your loving kindness and gentle corrections in our lives. Help me to embrace Your guidance and grow from the lessons You teach me each day. Amen.

True growth often comes from the soft whispers of correction rather than the loud cries of disappointment.

February 27

Hope That Will Not Disappoint

"And hope does not disappoint us, because God has poured out his love into our hearts by the Holy Spirit, whom he has given us." **Romans 5:5**

DEVOTIONAL

Embrace the small moments of hope in your life, for they are signs of God's unwavering love and promise for tomorrow.

DAILY REFLECTION

What does hope look like in your life right now, and how can you nurture it in your everyday moments?

PRAYER

Dear Lord, thank You for the gift of hope that shines through even in our darkest hours. Help us to hold on to that hope and share it with others, reminding us that we are never alone.

Hope is the light that fills our hearts
even when the path seems uncertain.

February 28

Becoming More Like Christ

"Therefore, as God's chosen people, holy and dearly loved, clothe yourselves with compassion, kindness, humility, gentleness, and patience."
Colossians 3:12

DEVOTIONAL

In seeking to become more like Christ, embrace the moments that challenge you as opportunities to reflect His character in your daily life.

DAILY REFLECTION

What does it look like for you to embody Christ's love in your everyday interactions with your family and friends?

PRAYER

Dear Lord, help me to reflect your love and grace in all that I do, especially in my role as a mother and friend. Guide my heart to mirror Your compassion and kindness to those around me.

To become more like Christ is to make love the center of every action.

March 1

When God Feels Silent

"Never will I leave you; never will I forsake you."
Hebrews 13:5

DEVOTIONAL

Sometimes, the silence we encounter isn't a sign of abandonment but a sacred space where God invites us to lean in closer and recognize His subtle workings in our lives.

DAILY REFLECTION

What do you feel in your heart when it seems like God is silent in your life? How can you draw closer to Him in this stillness?

PRAYER

Dear God, help me to find peace in moments of silence. Grant me the strength to trust in Your plan and embrace the stillness as I wait for Your guidance.

Even in silence, God is working behind the scenes; trust the process.

March 2

Becoming a Vessel of Grace

"Let your gentleness be evident to all. The Lord is near."
Philippians 4:5

DEVOTIONAL

The small acts of kindness and understanding you extend to your family and others around you are the echoes of grace that can transform not just their lives, but yours, too.

DAILY REFLECTION

What does it mean for you to be a vessel of grace in your daily life, especially in your roles as a mom, friend, and partner? How can you embody grace in your interactions today?

PRAYER

Dear God, help me to recognize the grace You have given me and empower me to extend that same grace to those around me. Fill my heart with compassion and understanding as I navigate my responsibilities today.

Becoming a vessel of grace is not a destination,
but a continuous journey of love and service.

March 3

Learning to Depend on Him

"Lord, you are my God; I will exalt you and praise your name, for in perfect faithfulness you have done wonderful things, things planned long ago."
Isaiah 25:1

DEVOTIONAL

Learning to lean on God allows us to embrace our vulnerabilities and discover that surrendering is not a sign of weakness but a gateway to His unfailing support and love.

DAILY REFLECTION

What areas of your life could you entrust more fully to God, and how might that change your daily experience? Consider the burdens you carry and how releasing them could open space for His guidance.

PRAYER

Dear Lord, help me to lean on You in my moments of uncertainty. Show me how to trust in Your plan and to feel Your presence in each step I take. Amen.

True strength is found in surrendering the weight of our worries to Him.

March 4

God's Timing Is Perfect

"For everything there is a season, a time for every activity under heaven."
Ecclesiastes 3:1

DEVOTIONAL

Trust in the beauty of God's timing, and know that every moment is an opportunity for growth and grace.

DAILY REFLECTION

What areas of your life are you waiting on God to move, and how can you shift your perspective to trust in His perfect timing?

PRAYER

Dear Lord, help me to embrace the moments of waiting in my life. Teach me to trust your perfect timing and fill my heart with peace as I navigate my journey.

Patience is not simply waiting: it's how we behave while we're waiting.

March 5

You Are Not Alone

*"Where can I go from your Spirit? Where can I flee from your presence? If I go up to the heavens, you are there; if I make my bed in the depths, you are there." **Psalm 139:7-10***

DEVOTIONAL

You are never alone; there are hearts around you that understand and share in your journey.

DAILY REFLECTION

What are the moments in your life when you've felt the strongest sense of solitude, and how has God's presence comforted you during these times?

PRAYER

Dear God, thank you for always being by my side, even during the hardest days. Help me to feel your presence and embrace the truth that I am never truly alone.

In the tapestry of life, the threads of solitude are woven with the presence of God's unwavering love.

March 6

Abiding in the Vine

*"I am the vine; you are the branches. If you remain in me and I in you, you will bear much fruit; apart from me, you can do nothing." **John 15:5***

DEVOTIONAL

In this season of life, remember that true strength and fruitfulness flow from your relationship with God; prioritize abiding in Him, and He will guide you through the busyness with grace and clarity.

DAILY REFLECTION

What does it mean for you to truly abide in Jesus amidst your daily responsibilities as a mother and friend? How can you cultivate a deeper connection with Him in the busyness of your life?

PRAYER

Dear God, thank You for being the true Vine in our lives. Help me to stay connected to You, drawing strength, love, and wisdom as I navigate my daily walk. May I find peace and joy in Your presence today.

Abiding in the Vine means finding strength in His love, especially when life feels overwhelming.

March 7

Trusting Through Transitions

"Commit your way to the Lord; trust in Him and He will act."
Psalm 37:5

DEVOTIONAL

Embracing life's transitions with trust can open doors to joy and fulfillment beyond what we can imagine.

DAILY REFLECTION

What transitions are currently unfolding in your life, and how can you embrace them while leaning into God's promises? How might you trust Him in these changes as a Mom and a woman navigating this beautiful yet complex season?

PRAYER

Dear God, thank you for being a constant in the midst of change. Help me to fully trust in Your plans as I navigate these transitions, and fill my heart with peace and clarity.

Trust is the bridge that carries you through the storm.

March 8

Choosing Peace in Uncertainty

"You will keep in perfect peace those whose minds are steadfast because they trust in you." **Isaiah 26:3**

DEVOTIONAL

Choose to embrace the peace that comes from trusting that you are not alone in your journey through uncertainty.

DAILY REFLECTION

What areas of your life feel uncertain right now, and how might choosing peace in those spaces transform your experience?

PRAYER

Dear God, in the midst of uncertainty, help me to find my anchor in You. Grant me the wisdom to choose peace over worry and to trust in Your guiding hand. Amen.

Peace is not the absence of chaos.
but the presence of tranquility in the midst of it.

March 9

Holding On to God's Promises

*"Your kingdom is an everlasting kingdom, and your dominion endures through all generations." **Psalm 145:13***

DEVOTIONAL

In the midst of life's uncertainties, God's promises are our anchor, guiding us through the storms of motherhood and beyond.

DAILY REFLECTION

What promises from God resonate with your heart today, and how can you hold on to them amid life's challenges? Reflect on the moments when His faithfulness has shone through, and consider how those experiences can strengthen your trust in Him now.

PRAYER

Dear Heavenly Father, thank you for your unwavering promises that sustain us in every season. Help me to cling to your truth and find comfort in your faithfulness, knowing that you are always with me.

God's promises are like anchors for our souls, steadying us through the storms of life.

March 10

Letting God Define Your Worth

*"Delight yourself in the Lord, and He will give you the desires of your heart." **Psalm 37:4***

DEVOTIONAL

You are cherished and defined by God's love, not the world's standards.

DAILY REFLECTION

What does it look like to let God define your worth in your daily life, especially as a mother and a woman navigating various roles and expectations? Reflect on the moments when you feel most valued and the source of that feeling.

PRAYER

Dear God, help me to see myself through Your eyes. Remind me of my intrinsic value in Your love, and guide me to let go of the world's definitions of worth. Amen.

Your worth is not defined by what you do, but by who you are in Christ.

March 11

Encouragement for the Weary Soul

"Come to me, all you who are weary and burdened, and I will give you rest."
Matthew 11:28

DEVOTIONAL

When you feel overwhelmed, don't hesitate to lay your burdens at God's feet, for He offers you rest and restoration.

DAILY REFLECTION

What burdens are you carrying today that feel heavy on your heart? How can you invite God's peace into those weary spaces of your soul?

PRAYER

Dear God, please wrap your loving arms around my weary soul today. Help me to find strength in you and peace in your presence as I navigate the challenges before me.

Even in our fatigue. His grace can become our refuge.

March 12

When You Feel Spiritually Stuck

"Do not conform to the pattern of this world, but be transformed by the renewing of your mind." **Romans 12:2**

DEVOTIONAL

In this season of your life, take time to prune away distractions and renew your spirit by embracing what nourishes your soul.

DAILY REFLECTION

What areas of your spiritual journey feel stagnant right now, and how might you invite God into those moments of struggle?

PRAYER

Dear Lord, please help me to find the courage to lean into my doubts and uncertainties. Remind me that you are always with me, even when I feel spiritually stuck.

Even in the stillness. God is working behind the scenes.

March 13

Faith That Moves Mountains

"If you have faith as small as a mustard seed, you can say to this mountain, 'Move from here to there,' and it will move. Nothing will be impossible for you." Matthew 17:20

DEVOTIONAL

Whatever mountains loom in your life, trust that your faith, no matter how small, has the power to transform your circumstances.

DAILY REFLECTION

What mountains are you facing in your life right now? How is your faith guiding you through these challenges?

PRAYER

Dear God, thank You for the strength You provide us through our faith. Help us to trust that, with You, we can overcome every mountain in our path. Amen.

Faith is not the absence of fear but the assurance that God is bigger than any challenge we face.

March 14

The Gentle Voice of God

"In the stillness, you will hear His whisper, guiding you through the complexities of life." 1 Kings 19:12

DEVOTIONAL

Trust that in the busyness of life, God's voice is often soft, calling you back to moments of peace and clarity.

DAILY REFLECTION

What whispers of comfort or guidance is God gently sharing with you today, amidst the noise of your busy life? Can you pause for a moment to hear Him?

PRAYER

Dear God, thank you for your gentle voice that calms our hearts and directs our paths. Help me to slow down and intentionally listen for Your guidance in my daily life.

In the stillness of the heart, we often find God's softest whisper.

March 15

Living with Kingdom Vision

"But seek first the kingdom of God and His righteousness, and all these things shall be added to you." **Matthew 6:33**

DEVOTIONAL

In this season of life, remember that your purpose extends beyond daily tasks; embracing your role in God's kingdom can breathe new life into your journey.

DAILY REFLECTION

What does it look like for you to embrace your role as a daughter of the King in your daily life? How can you align your decisions and interactions with the values of His Kingdom?

PRAYER

Dear Lord, guide this woman as she navigates her daily challenges. Help her to see the beauty in each moment and to reflect Your love and grace in all that she does. May she find strength and courage through Your promise.

Living with Kingdom Vision invites us to see our lives through the lens of purpose and grace, illuminating every moment with the light of His love.

March 16

Standing Firm in Faith

"Otherwise, would they not have stopped being offered? For the worshipers would have been cleansed once for all, and would no longer have felt guilty for their sins." **Hebrews 10:23**

DEVOTIONAL

The journey of motherhood and faith teaches us to be resilient; embrace the challenges knowing they shape not just your children, but your spirit as well.

DAILY REFLECTION

What areas of your life are calling for a steadfast faith today, and how can you trust God more fully in those moments?

PRAYER

Dear Lord, please grant her a heart that remains strong and steadfast, embracing the journey of faith with courage and hope. Surround her with Your love, reminding her that she is never alone.

Faith is not the absence of doubt, but the determination to trust God amidst it.

March 17

Letting Go of Shame

"Brothers and sisters, I do not consider myself yet to have taken hold of it. But one thing I do: Forgetting what is behind and straining toward what is ahead, I press on toward the goal to win the prize for which God has called me heavenward in Christ Jesus." **Philippians 3:13-14**

DEVOTIONAL

You are not defined by your past, but by the grace that guides you toward a brighter future.

DAILY REFLECTION

What are the moments in your life where you've felt shame, and how might letting go of those feelings transform your heart and relationships?

PRAYER

Dear God, help me to release the burdens of shame that I have carried. May Your love show me the way to healing and renewal, embracing the truth that I am enough just as I am.

Shame can weigh us down, but grace lifts us up.

March 18

Anchored in His Word

"We have this hope as an anchor for the soul, firm and secure. It enters the inner sanctuary behind the curtain." **Hebrews 6:19**

DEVOTIONAL

When the waves of chaos crash around you, remember that God's Word is your steadfast anchor, providing strength and direction for the journey ahead.

DAILY REFLECTION

What does it look like in your daily life to be anchored in God's Word, especially when faced with challenges as a mom?

PRAYER

Dear God, thank You for Your unwavering presence in our lives. Help me to find solace and strength in Your Word each day, guiding me to be a light for my family and those around me.

When we are anchored in His Word,
our souls find peace amidst life's storms.

March 19

Brave in the Small Things

"When I am afraid, I put my trust in you, in God, whose word I praise— in God I trust and am not afraid. What can mere mortals do to me?"
Psalm 56:3-4

DEVOTIONAL

Every act of love and attention in our lives, no matter how small, embodies a kind of bravery that shapes our families and ourselves.

DAILY REFLECTION

What small act of courage can you embrace today that might lead to a greater impact in your life or the lives of those around you?

PRAYER

Dear God, help me to recognize the bravery required in the small moments of my day. Grant me the strength to act with love and to approach each situation with a courageous heart.

Small acts of bravery can illuminate the path to larger victories.

March 20

Your Pain Has a Purpose

"When you pass through the waters, I will be with you; and when you pass through the rivers, they will not sweep over you." **Isaiah 43:2**

DEVOTIONAL

Your pain, dear sister, is not without purpose; it is molding you into the woman you are meant to be, equipped to nurture and guide those around you.

DAILY REFLECTION

What pain in your life has shaped you the most, and how can you see that struggle as part of your journey toward purpose? Reflect on what lessons you've learned along the way.

PRAYER

Dear God, thank you for walking with me through my pain. Help me to see the purpose behind my struggles and to trust that you are using them to mold me into the woman I am meant to be.

Even in the darkest valleys,
your scars have the power to illuminate your purpose.

March 21

A God Who Redeems

"So if the Son sets you free, you will be free indeed."
John 8:36

DEVOTIONAL

Your story, like Sarah's, is a testament to the wonderful ways God redeems our experiences, inviting you to trust that every chapter is woven into a beautiful tapestry of grace.

DAILY REFLECTION

What areas of your life do you feel need redemption right now, and how can you invite God into those situations?

PRAYER

Dear God, thank You for always being present in our lives, ready to redeem our past and reshape our future. Help us to trust in Your loving hand as we seek healing and renewal in our hearts and homes.

Redemption isn't just a one-time event;
it's a beautiful process of transformation and grace.

March 22

Becoming Spiritually Resilient

"Be strong and courageous. Do not be afraid; do not be discouraged, for the Lord your God will be with you wherever you go." **Joshua 1:9**

DEVOTIONAL

Trust that even in the changes of life, God is nurturing your resilience and guiding your heart through every season.

DAILY REFLECTION

What moments in your life have tested your faith, and how have you found strength in those challenging times?

PRAYER

Dear God, help me to recognize the lessons in my trials. May my faith be strengthened and my heart remain open to Your guidance as I strive to be spiritually resilient.

Strength does not come from what you can do; it comes from overcoming the things you once thought you couldn't.

March 23

Overflowing with Living Water

*"Whoever believes in me, as Scripture has said, rivers of living water will flow from within them." **John 7:38***

DEVOTIONAL

As you navigate the beautiful, yet sometimes exhausting, journey of motherhood and life, remember that God desires to fill you with His living water, so that you may overflow with love, grace, and joy.

DAILY REFLECTION

What are the sources you turn to for refreshment and nourishment in your life, and how can you ensure they are filled with the Living Water that never runs dry?

PRAYER

Dear God, thank You for being the source of Living Water in our lives. Help us to seek You daily and fill us with the peace and joy that comes from Your presence.

When our hearts are filled with Your love,
we can pour out that love onto our families and communities.

March 24

Choosing Rest Over Rush

*"Come to me, all you who are weary and burdened, and I will give you rest." **Luke 11:28***

DEVOTIONAL

In the midst of the whirlwind of motherhood and daily responsibilities, remember that taking time to rest is not about neglecting duties but embracing the sacred act of self-care, allowing ourselves to recharge and be present for those we love.

DAILY REFLECTION

What in your life feels rushed right now, and how can you intentionally create space for rest amidst the demands of motherhood and daily responsibilities?

PRAYER

Dear God, please help me embrace moments of stillness in the chaos of my life. Teach me to prioritize rest and to find Your peace in the midst of my busyness. Amen.

Rest is not the absence of work; it's the presence of peace.

March 25

A Heart That Seeks God

"Blessed are those who keep his statutes and seek him with all their heart."
Psalm 119:2

DEVOTIONAL

No matter how chaotic life becomes, carving out time for God can transform our hearts and minds, bringing us the clarity and peace we seek.

DAILY REFLECTION

What does it look like in your day-to-day life to actively seek God's presence and guidance? Are there moments you can identify where you felt a nudge to draw closer to Him?

PRAYER

Dear God, guide my heart and mind as I seek You today. Help me to recognize Your presence in the simple moments and to trust in Your plan for my life. Amen.

A heart that seeks God finds peace amidst the chaos of life.

March 26

Obedience in the Little Things

"Well done, good and faithful servant; you have been faithful over a little; I will set you over much." **Matthew 25:21**

DEVOTIONAL

The little things matter, and in moments of obedience to those small nudges, we may uncover profound blessings in our lives and the lives of others.

DAILY REFLECTION

What are some small acts of obedience in your daily life that you might be overlooking, and how can embracing them change your outlook or influence those around you?

PRAYER

Dear Lord, help me to recognize and embrace the small moments of obedience in my day. Thank You for guiding me gently towards Your will in my life.

Obedience in the little things opens the door to greater blessings.

March 27

The Gift of Quiet Moments

"Come to me, all you who are weary and burdened, and I will give you rest."
Matthew 11:28-30

DEVOTIONAL

Embrace the gift of quiet moments; they are where your heart can find peace and your spirit can be rejuvenated.

DAILY REFLECTION

What does it feel like for you to carve out those quiet moments in your day? How can you intentionally embrace stillness amid the busy rhythms of motherhood and life?

PRAYER

Dear God, thank you for the gift of quiet moments amidst our busy lives. Help me to recognize and savor these times, knowing they are precious treasures that draw me closer to You.

In the stillness, we often hear the whispers of our hearts.

March 28

He Carries Your Burdens

"Cast all your anxiety on him because he cares for you."
1 Peter 5:7

DEVOTIONAL

Life teaches us that sharing our worries with God can bring profound relief, reminding us that we do not have to navigate our challenges alone.

DAILY REFLECTION

What burdens are you carrying today that you need to lay down at His feet?

PRAYER

Dear Lord, thank you for being our source of strength. Help me to trust in You as I cast my cares upon You, knowing You are always here to carry my burdens.

Let Him lighten your load, for He is always ready to lift you up.

March 29

Your Journey Is Sacred

"The Lord directs the steps of the godly. He delights in every detail of their lives. Though they stumble, they will never fall, for the Lord holds them by the hand." **Psalm 37:23-24**

DEVOTIONAL

Your journey, with all its ups and downs, is a sacred tapestry woven by divine intent, leading you closer to your true self.

DAILY REFLECTION

What moments in your life have felt particularly sacred, and how can you nurture that sense of holiness in your daily routine?

PRAYER

Dear God, thank You for the gift of this journey. Help me to see the beauty and purpose in every step, and grant me the wisdom to honor the sacredness of my life.

Your journey is a tapestry woven with divine threads, each experience adding depth and beauty to your story.

March 30

Victory in Christ

"In this world, you will have trouble. But take heart! I have overcome the world." **John 16:33**

DEVOTIONAL

Every small triumph in your life, whether it's getting through a long day or nurturing your family, is a reminder of the greater victory found in Christ.

DAILY REFLECTION

What victories have you experienced in your life where you know it was Christ who carried you through? Reflect on those moments and how they have shaped your journey as a mom and as a woman of faith.

PRAYER

Dear Lord, thank You for the victories You have given us through Christ. Help us to recognize and celebrate these moments in our lives, trusting in Your strength and guidance each step of the way.

In Christ, every battle is an opportunity for breakthrough.

March 31

Renewal in Christ

"And He who sits on the throne said, 'Behold, I am making all things new.'" **Revelation 21:5**

DEVOTIONAL

In the midst of life's changes, remember that God is always working to make you new, shaping your heart and spirit for each season He brings.

DAILY REFLECTION

What in your life feels worn or in need of renewal, and how can you invite Christ into those spaces today?

PRAYER

Dear Lord, thank You for the gift of renewal through Your love. Help me to embrace the changes You bring, knowing that in every season, I am held by Your grace.

Just as spring brings new blooms after a long winter, Christ offers us a fresh start filled with hope and purpose.

April 1

When You Need Reassurance

"The name of the Lord is a fortified tower; the righteous run to it and are safe." **Proverbs 18:10**

DEVOTIONAL

Even in the chaos of life and uncertainty, turning to God provides a stronghold of peace and reassurance.

DAILY REFLECTION

What is it in your life that feels uncertain or overwhelming right now, and how can you remind yourself of joy and hope in the midst of those feelings?

PRAYER

Dear God, thank You for being our constant source of comfort and strength. Please help me to open my heart to Your reassurance and to trust in Your plans for my life, even when the path feels unclear.

Amid the storms of life, His whispers of love carry the promise of peace.

April 2

Rooted in God's Word

"But whose delight is in the law of the Lord, and who meditates on his law day and night. That person is like a tree planted by streams of water, which yields its fruit in season and whose leaf does not wither—whatever they do prospers." **Psalm 1:2-3**

DEVOTIONAL

When we take time to immerse ourselves in God's Word, we anchor our hearts, allowing us to thrive even in life's storms.

DAILY REFLECTION

What are some ways you can deepen your connection to God's Word in your daily life, and how might that transform your role as a mom and woman of faith?

PRAYER

Dear God, thank you for the richness of your Word that nourishes my spirit. Help me to open my heart and mind to your teachings, guiding me as I strive to embody your love in my family and community.

Rooted in God's Word, we flourish like trees planted by streams of water, bearing fruit in every season.

April 3

Faith for the Future

"And my God will meet all your needs according to the riches of his glory in Christ Jesus." **Philippians 4:19**

DEVOTIONAL

Sometimes, embracing the uncertainty of the future is the key to discovering the depth of your faith.

DAILY REFLECTION

What dreams or plans for the future have you set aside, and how can you bring your faith alongside them today?

PRAYER

Dear God, as I journey into the future, I ask for your guidance and strength. Help me to trust in your plans, knowing they are crafted with love and purpose. Fill my heart with hope as I step into each new day.

Faith is not just a belief: it's the courage to step forward even when the path is unclear.

April 4

Choosing Joy Daily

"Consider it pure joy, my sisters, whenever you face trials of many kinds, because you know that the testing of your faith produces perseverance." **James 1:2-3**

DEVOTIONAL

In the daily grind, remember that joy is not just a feeling but a choice you can make, even when circumstances seem less than ideal. By recognizing the small moments of beauty and grace in your life, you cultivate a heart that chooses to rejoice, creating a ripple effect of positivity for yourself and your family.

DAILY REFLECTION

What small changes can you make today to intentionally choose joy in your daily routine? How can you cultivate moments of happiness amidst your responsibilities?

PRAYER

Dear God, thank You for the gift of today. Help me to see the beauty in the ordinary and to embrace joy even in the midst of my busy life. May Your presence fill my heart and guide my steps toward a joyful spirit.

Joy is not the absence of challenges but the presence of gratitude in all circumstances.

April 5

God's Presence in the Waiting

"I waited patiently for the Lord; he turned to me and heard my cry. He lifted me out of the slimy pit, out of the mud and mire; he set my feet on a rock and gave me a firm place to stand. He put a new song in my mouth, a hymn of praise to our God." **Psalm 40:1-3**

DEVOTIONAL

In the seasons of waiting, trust that you are never alone; God's presence is there, guiding you toward His perfect plan.

DAILY REFLECTION

What areas of your life feel like they're on pause right now, and how can you invite God to be present with you in that waiting?

PRAYER

Dear God, thank You for being with us in every season of our lives, especially during the moments of waiting. Help us to feel Your comforting presence as we navigate this journey, trusting that You are at work in ways we may not yet see.

God's silence does not mean He is absent; it often means He is preparing us for something more beautiful.

April 6

A Heart of Humility

"Humble yourselves before the Lord, and he will lift you up."
James 4:10

DEVOTIONAL

In embracing humility, we discover that true strength lies not in always having the answers, but in being present for others and allowing our hearts to grow through their journeys.

DAILY REFLECTION

What does it look like in your daily life to embrace a heart of humility, especially as a mom balancing so many roles? Are there moments when pride creeps in, and how can you gently redirect your heart towards humility?

PRAYER

Dear Lord, thank you for the gift of motherhood and the lessons it brings. Help me cultivate a heart of humility that reflects your love and grace, even in the busiest moments. May I learn to lift others up and delight in their successes alongside my own.

Humility opens the door to deeper connections and enriches the fabric of our relationships.

April 7

Walking in God's Strength

"Be strong and courageous. Do not be afraid; do not be discouraged, for the Lord your God will be with you wherever you go." **Deuteronomy 31:6**

DEVOTIONAL

Even in our busiest and most overwhelming moments, God invites us to lean on Him for the strength we need to keep moving forward.

DAILY REFLECTION

What are some situations in your life where you feel you need God's strength the most right now, and how can you invite Him into those moments?

PRAYER

Dear God, thank you for being our source of strength and comfort. Help me to lean on You in moments of uncertainty and to trust that You are with me every step of the way.

God's strength is a gentle reminder that we are never alone in our struggles.

April 8

Compassion Like Christ

"When He saw the crowds, He had compassion for them, because they were harassed and helpless, like sheep without a shepherd." **Matthew 9:36**

DEVOTIONAL

Look for opportunities to show compassion, as your kindness can breathe life into someone who may be silently suffering.

DAILY REFLECTION

What are some ways you can show compassion in your daily interactions, embracing the gentle heart of Christ? Consider how small acts might transform not only others' lives but your own as well.

PRAYER

Dear God, thank You for showing us love and compassion through Your Son, Jesus. Help me to reflect that same compassion in my daily life, seeking to lift up those around me.

Compassion is often the quiet response of the heart that sees the struggles of others and chooses to love unconditionally.

April 9

Overcoming Spiritual Burnout

"Therefore encourage one another and build each other up, just as in fact you are doing." **1 Thessalonians 5:11**

DEVOTIONAL

Embrace small moments of solitude to refill your spirit; they are essential for your journey.

DAILY REFLECTION

What areas of your spiritual life feel depleted or overwhelming, and how can you invite God to refresh and renew those aspects?

PRAYER

Dear God, please fill me with Your peace and strength as I navigate the challenges of life. Help me to slow down and seek Your presence amid the busyness, finding rest for my soul in You.

Even in the midst of chaos, His love is an oasis to the weary.

April 10

The Hope of the Resurrection

"Praise be to the God and Father of our Lord Jesus Christ! In his great mercy, he has given us new birth into a living hope through the resurrection of Jesus Christ from the dead." **1 Peter 1:3**

DEVOTIONAL

This week, remember that even in life's darkest moments, the hope of the resurrection assures you that there is always the potential for renewal and brighter days ahead.

DAILY REFLECTION

What does the hope of the resurrection mean to you in your everyday life, and how does it shape your perspective on challenges you face as a mother and woman?

PRAYER

Dear God, thank you for the promise of new life and the hope that comes through the resurrection. Help me to embody that hope in my daily challenges and to share it abundantly with those around me.

*From the ashes of disappointment,
new life can blossom through the promise of resurrection.*

April 11

Pouring Out, Being Filled

"The Lord will guide you continually, and satisfy your soul in drought, and strengthen your bones; you shall be like a watered garden, and like a spring of water, whose waters do not fail." *Isaiah 58:11*

DEVOTIONAL

True replenishment comes not only from the act of giving but also from intentionally creating space in our lives to receive God's love and grace.

DAILY REFLECTION

What areas of your life feel drained or empty, and where might God be inviting you to pour out His love and grace?

PRAYER

Dear Lord, fill us with Your Spirit as we pour ourselves out for our families and communities. Help us to find joy in serving others while also allowing ourselves to be refilled with Your love. Amen.

In our moments of giving, we discover the depths of our own hearts being replenished.

April 12

God's Provision Is Enough

"So don't worry about these things, saying, 'What will we eat? What will we drink? What will we wear?' These things dominate the thoughts of unbelievers, but your heavenly Father already knows all your needs. Seek the Kingdom of God above all else, and live righteously, and he will give you everything you need." *Matthew 6:31–33*

DEVOTIONAL

Even in the midst of chaos and uncertainty, trust that God's provision always arrives, often dressed in the form of everyday blessings.

DAILY REFLECTION

What areas of your life feel uncertain, and how can you invite God into those spaces to truly trust in His provision today?

PRAYER

Dear God, thank You for always being faithful and providing for us in our times of need. Help me to recognize Your blessings and trust that Your provision is enough for every challenge I face.

God's provision meets our needs, even when we cannot see the path ahead.

April 13

Women of Purpose

"She is clothed with strength and dignity; she can laugh at the days to come. She speaks with wisdom, and faithful instruction is on her tongue."
Proverbs 31:25-26

DEVOTIONAL

You are not just a caretaker; your unique talents and passions are vital to the world and deserve to be explored and celebrated.

DAILY REFLECTION

What does it mean for you to live with purpose in this season of your life, and how can you embrace the unique gifts and insights you bring to the world?

PRAYER

Dear God, please help me to understand the purpose you have woven into the fabric of my life. Guide me as I navigate my responsibilities and dreams, reminding me that I am valued and cherished in your sight.

Your purpose is not just a destination; it's the journey of becoming all that you were meant to be.

April 14

Courage to Begin Again

"For I am confident of this very thing, that He who began a good work in you will perfect it until the day of Christ Jesus." **Philippians 1:6**

DEVOTIONAL

Courage is not the absence of fear; it is the willingness to take the first step, regardless of how daunting it may seem.

DAILY REFLECTION

What does "beginning again" look like for you in this season of your life? What fears or doubts might be holding you back from stepping into new opportunities or changes?

PRAYER

Dear God, give me the courage to embrace fresh starts with an open heart. Help me to trust in Your plan for my life as I step boldly into new beginnings. Amen.

Every day is a new opportunity to rise from the ashes of yesterday's disappointments and create something beautiful.

April 15

Faithful in the Hidden Places

"But when you pray, go into your room and shut the door and pray to your Father who is in secret. And your Father who sees in secret will reward you."
Matthew 6:6

DEVOTIONAL

The most profound growth in faith often happens in the quiet, hidden places where we meet God in prayer and reflection.

DAILY REFLECTION

What are the hidden places in your life where you feel God is calling you to be faithful, even when no one is watching?

PRAYER

Dear Lord, thank you for being present in the quiet moments of our lives. Help me embrace the hidden places with grace and faith, trusting in Your perfect timing and purpose.

True strength is revealed in the diligent care of what seems insignificant.

April 16

Living Light in a Heavy World

"Therefore, since we are surrounded by such a great cloud of witnesses, let us throw off everything that hinders and the sin that so easily entangles. And let us run with perseverance the race marked out for us, fixing our eyes on Jesus, the pioneer and perfecter of faith. For the joy set before him he endured the cross, scorning its shame, and sat down at the right hand of the throne of God." **Hebrews 12:1-2**

DEVOTIONAL

In a world heavy with demands, remember to create space for joy and gratitude amidst the clutter of life.

DAILY REFLECTION

What burdens are you carrying today that keep you from feeling the lightness of God's love? How might you invite Him to help you let go of them?

PRAYER

Dear God, thank You for Your light that shines even in the darkest places. Help me to release the heavy burdens I've been carrying and to embrace the freedom and joy found in Your presence.

Lightness comes not from the absence of weight, but from the presence of grace.

April 17

Trusting God with the Unknown

*"You will keep in perfect peace those whose minds are steadfast because they trust in you. Trust in the Lord forever, for the Lord, the Lord himself, is the Rock eternal." **Isaiah 26:3-4***

DEVOTIONAL

Life often feels like an unfolding tapestry where we can only see a portion of the picture; trusting God means recognizing that He holds the full design and will never lead us astray.

DAILY REFLECTION

What unknowns are you currently facing that require a leap of faith, and how might you invite God into those uncertainties?

PRAYER

Dear Lord, help me to release my worries about the future into Your loving hands. Grant me the courage to trust in Your plan, even when the path ahead feels unclear.

*Faith is not about knowing the future,
but trusting the One who holds it.*

April 18

Embracing God's Refining

"For you, O God, have tested us; you have tried us as silver is tried."
Psalm 66:10

DEVOTIONAL

Embrace the refining process, for through it we emerge stronger and more radiant in our God-given identity.

DAILY REFLECTION

What areas of your life feel in need of God's refining touch right now, and how can you invite Him into those moments?

PRAYER

Dear God, thank You for the promise of Your steadfast love and the work You do within us. Help me to embrace the challenges of my life as opportunities for growth and transformation. Amen.

Through the fire, He shapes us into vessels of His grace.

April 19

Gratitude in the Grind

"Give thanks to the Lord, for He is good; His love endures forever."
Psalm 107:1

DEVOTIONAL

Every effort you make to nurture your family holds beauty; find gratitude in the midst of your busy days, for those small moments of joy are the heartbeat of your journey.

DAILY REFLECTION

What are the little moments in your daily grind that you can choose to be grateful for today, even amidst the chaos of motherhood and daily responsibilities?

PRAYER

Dear God, thank you for the gift of today. Help me to see and cherish the beauty in the ordinary moments, even when life feels overwhelming.

*Gratitude transforms the messiness of life
into a tapestry of precious moments.*

April 20

Holding On to Hope

"Hope deferred makes the heart sick, but a longing fulfilled is a tree of life."
Proverbs 13:12

DEVOTIONAL

Sometimes, hope comes alive in the smallest of moments, teaching us to cherish what we have while patiently waiting for the dreams that still lie ahead.

DAILY REFLECTION

What are the hopes you hold on to in your heart, and how can you nurture them through life's challenges? Consider the dreams that ignite your spirit and those that might feel out of reach.

PRAYER

Dear God, thank you for the gift of hope and the promise that you are always with us. Help us to embrace our dreams and trust in Your perfect timing as we navigate life's journey.

Hope is the quiet certainty that blooms even in the harshest seasons.

April 21

God's Still Small Voice

"...a time to tear and a time to mend, a time to be silent and a time to speak,..." **Ecclesiastes 3:7**

DEVOTIONAL

Embrace the quiet moments in your day; they are often where you will hear God's voice most clearly.

DAILY REFLECTION

What is one moment this week where you can pause and listen for God's still small voice in the midst of your busy life?

PRAYER

Dear Lord, help me to quiet my heart and mind so I can hear Your gentle whispers amid the chaos of daily life. Guide me to embrace the peace that comes from Your presence.

In the silence, we often find the clearest answers.

April 22

The Beauty of Forgiveness

"Bear with each other and forgive one another if any of you has a grievance against someone. Forgive as the Lord forgave you."
Colossians 3:13

DEVOTIONAL

Forgiveness is a gift we give not only to others but to ourselves, liberating us from the burdens that weigh down our spirits.

DAILY REFLECTION

What does forgiveness look like in your life, and how can embracing it uplift your spirit and relationships? Think about someone you might be holding onto resentment towards. How might healing those wounds change your heart?

PRAYER

Dear God, help me to cultivate a heart of forgiveness. May I find the courage to release grudges and embrace the freedom that comes from letting go. Fill me with your peace as I take this journey.

Forgiveness is the gentle grace that transforms our scars into stories of strength.

April 23

When You Feel Spiritually Empty

"The human spirit can endure in sickness, but a crushed spirit who can bear?" **Proverbs 18:14**

DEVOTIONAL

Even in the midst of life's demands, take intentional moments to replenish your spirit, for it is in those quiet spaces that you can reconnect with God and find renewal.

DAILY REFLECTION

What does it feel like for you when your spirit feels empty, and how can you invite God's presence back into your life during those moments?

PRAYER

Dear God, in times of spiritual emptiness, may I feel your loving arms around me. Fill my heart with your peace and renew my spirit as I seek your presence each day.

Even in our emptiest moments, God is just a prayer away, waiting to fill us with His grace.

April 24

Peace That Transcends

"Peace I leave with you; my peace I give you. I do not give to you as the world gives. Do not let your hearts be troubled and do not be afraid."
John 14:27

DEVOTIONAL

Embrace the moments of stillness amidst your busyness—it's in those spaces where God's transcendent peace can refresh your spirit.

DAILY REFLECTION

What weighs on your heart that keeps you from experiencing the peace you long for? Can you identify moments when you've felt a peace that transcended your circumstances? How can you invite that peace into your life today?

PRAYER

Dear God, help me find your peace that surpasses all understanding. May I feel your presence in every moment, calming my heart and guiding my thoughts. Amen.

True peace is not the absence of chaos but the presence of God.

April 25

Carrying God's Light

*"But the fruit of the Spirit is love, joy, peace, forbearance, kindness, goodness, faithfulness, gentleness and self-control. Against such things there is no law." **Galatians 5:22-23***

DEVOTIONAL

You are a beacon of light in your home, illuminating the lives of those around you with love and kindness, even during the ordinary moments.

DAILY REFLECTION

What does it mean to you to carry God's light into your daily life, especially as a wife and mother? How can you reflect that light in your interactions with your family and the world around you?

PRAYER

Dear Lord, thank You for the light You have placed within me. Help me to shine this light brightly in my home and in all my interactions, reflecting Your love and grace to those around me.

Your light is a beacon of hope; let it shine in every corner of your life.

April 26

Standing on God's Promises

"The one who calls you is faithful, and he will do it."
1 Thessalonians 5:24

DEVOTIONAL

Always remember that standing on God's promises means trusting that His plans for you are far greater than your worries.

DAILY REFLECTION

What promises of God are you standing on today, and how do they guide your daily choices and priorities?

PRAYER

Dear Lord, thank You for Your steadfast promises that never fail. Help me to trust in Your plans and to find strength in the assurance of Your unfailing love and guidance each day.

Standing on God's promises means finding peace in uncertainty and hope in every challenge.

April 27

Finding Rest in His Love

"For I am convinced that neither death nor life, neither angels nor demons, neither the present nor the future, nor any powers, neither height nor depth, nor anything else in all creation, will be able to separate us from the love of God that is in Christ Jesus our Lord." **Romans 8:38–39**

DEVOTIONAL

In moments of overwhelm, remember that His unending love is your true source of rest and strength.

DAILY REFLECTION

What does it mean for you to find rest in God's love amidst your busy life as a mom? Can you identify moments in your day when you can pause and soak in that love?

PRAYER

Dear God, thank You for Your endless love that surrounds us. Help me to slow down and lean into that love, finding peace in Your presence every day. Amen.

Rest is not found in the busyness of our tasks.
but in the embrace of His unwavering love.

April 28

Walking by Faith, Not Sight

"For we walk by faith, not by sight."
2 Corinthians 5:7

DEVOTIONAL

Sometimes, we need to let go of our need for certainty and embrace the unknown, remembering that faith is our guiding light through every season of life.

DAILY REFLECTION

What are the areas in your life where you find it difficult to trust God fully? How can you take steps to rely more on your faith rather than what you see around you?

PRAYER

Dear God, help me to embrace faith over fear as I navigate life's uncertainties. Strengthen my heart to trust in Your goodness, even when I can't see the path ahead.

Faith is taking the first step
even when you don't see the whole staircase.

April 29

God's Grace Through Every Season

"My flesh and my heart may fail, but God is the strength of my heart and my portion forever." **Psalm 73:26**

DEVOTIONAL

Even in the most chaotic seasons of life, remember that God's grace is a gentle umbrella of strength and refuge that shelters you, guiding you toward peace and renewal.

DAILY REFLECTION

What seasons have you experienced in your life that have challenged your perception of God's grace? How might your understanding of His presence shift during those times?

PRAYER

Dear God, thank You for Your unwavering grace that follows us through every season of life. Help us to recognize Your loving presence and embrace the beauty You bring, even in difficult times.

God's grace is like a warm blanket, comforting and protective, wrapping us in love during every storm.

April 30

Grace for Today

"For by grace you have been saved through faith, and that not of yourselves; it is the gift of God, not of works, lest anyone should boast." **Ephesians 2:8-9**

DEVOTIONAL

Grace is an ongoing gift that enables us to embrace our imperfections and those of our loved ones, reminding us to approach each day with open hearts.

DAILY REFLECTION

What are the moments in your day today where you can pause and recognize God's grace at work, even in the small things?

PRAYER

Dear God, thank You for Your unwavering grace that sustains me each day. Help me to see Your hand in my life and to share that grace generously with my family and friends.

Grace is not just a gift we receive; it's a way we live every moment.

May 1

Becoming a Prayerful Woman

"Pray without ceasing."
1 Thessalonians 5:17

DEVOTIONAL

In cultivating a prayerful heart, we learn that even the simplest conversations with God can nourish our souls and ground us in His presence.

DAILY REFLECTION

What does a prayerful life look like for you, and how can you nurture that relationship with God in your busy days?

PRAYER

Dear Lord, as I navigate the complexities of life, remind me to turn to You in prayer. Help me cultivate a heart that seeks You first and finds peace in Your presence.

*Prayer is not just asking: it is listening for
the whisper of God in the midst of our busy lives.*

May 2

God's Strength in Your Story

*"Fear not, for I have redeemed you;
I have called you by name, you are mine."* **Isaiah 43:1**

DEVOTIONAL

Even in the midst of chaos, God's strength is the quiet foundation that holds our stories together.

DAILY REFLECTION

What challenges are you facing today where you need to feel God's strength in your story? How can you invite Him into those moments to reveal His power in your life?

PRAYER

Dear Father, thank You for being a constant source of strength and comfort. Help us to lean on You today, trusting that Your power is at work in our stories, even when we feel weak. Amen.

*Your story is a tapestry woven with threads of grace and strength.
where every challenge has a purpose and every victory.
no matter how small. is a testament to His love.*

May 3

Restoring Your Soul

"He refreshes my soul. He guides me along the right paths for His name's sake." **Psalm 23:3**

DEVOTIONAL

Restoration begins when you acknowledge your need for it and prioritize moments of peace in your busy life.

DAILY REFLECTION

What does your soul long for in this season of your life, and how can you create space to nurture that need each day?

PRAYER

Dear God, help me embrace the quiet moments where my soul can find rest. Restore in me a sense of peace and joy that rejuvenates my spirit and nourishes my heart. Amen.

In the stillness, your soul whispers what it truly needs.

May 4

Trusting God in the Unknown

"But now, this is what the Lord says, He who created you, O Jacob, and He who formed you, O Israel: Do not fear, for I have redeemed you; I have called you by name; you are Mine. When you pass through the waters, I will be with you, and through the rivers, they will not overwhelm you; when you walk through the fire, you will not be scorched, nor will the flame burn you." **Isaiah 43:1-2**

DEVOTIONAL

Trusting God in our uncertainties often opens up pathways we never imagined possible, revealing strengths and resilience we didn't know we had.

DAILY REFLECTION

What areas of your life right now feel uncertain, and how can you invite God into those spaces? What does trusting Him look like for you in the midst of the unknown?

PRAYER

Dear God, as I navigate the uncertain paths before me, help me to rest in Your promises and lean on Your understanding. Fill my heart with peace as I trust in Your perfect timing and plan for my life.

Faith is not about knowing the future; it's about trusting the One who holds it.

May 5

Overflowing with Compassion

"...because judgment without mercy will be shown to anyone who has not been merciful. Mercy triumphs over judgment..." **James 2:13**

DEVOTIONAL

Compassion, when practiced, not only uplifts others but also fills our own hearts with purpose and joy "

DAILY REFLECTION

What does compassion look like in your everyday life, and how can you extend that to your family and community today?

PRAYER

Dear God, help me to see the needs of those around me and to offer my heart with open arms. Fill me with Your love so that I may overflow with compassion for others.

Compassion is not just feeling for others;
it's actively engaging to bring comfort and hope.

May 6

The Power of a Grateful Heart

"Give thanks in all circumstances; for this is the will of God in Christ Jesus for you." **1 Thessalonians 5:18**

DEVOTIONAL

Choose to nurture a grateful heart, for it has the power to illuminate your path and help you appreciate the abundant blessings in your life.

DAILY REFLECTION

What are three things you're grateful for today, and how can acknowledging those gifts shift your perspective in the moments of this busy season?

PRAYER

Dear God, thank you for the countless blessings in our lives. Help us to see and cherish the small miracles that surround us each day. Fill our hearts with gratitude and let it overflow into our actions.

A grateful heart sees the beauty in even the ordinary moments.

May 7

Faith in the Storm

"Now faith is confidence in what we hope for and assurance about what we do not see." **Hebrews 11:1**

DEVOTIONAL

When the storms of life rage, remember that your faith is not only your refuge but also a powerful force that can guide you through the toughest times.

DAILY REFLECTION

What storms are you currently facing in your life, and how can you invite God into those turbulent moments for comfort and guidance?

PRAYER

Dear God, in the midst of life's storms, help me to trust in Your presence. Calm my heart and fill me with hope as I navigate through the waves that threaten to overwhelm me.

*Faith doesn't eliminate the storm;
it assures us of the anchor we have in the midst of it.*

May 8

When You Feel Invisible

"For we are God's masterpiece. He has created us anew in Christ Jesus, so we can do the good things he planned for us long ago." **Ephesians 2:10**

DEVOTIONAL

Remember, even in moments when you feel unseen, you are a precious creation with gifts and potential only you can fulfill.

DAILY REFLECTION

What moments in your life do you feel unseen or overlooked, and how can you invite God into those feelings today?

PRAYER

Dear God, help me to recognize my worth in Your eyes and remind me that I am never truly invisible to You. May Your love fill my heart and grant me peace in the moments when I feel ignored or unnoticed.

*In the silent corners of life, His presence whispers,
reminding us that we are known and cherished.*

May 9

Rooted in God's Love

"But the love of the Lord remains forever with those who fear him. His salvation extends to the children's children " **Psalm 103:17**

DEVOTIONAL

In every season of motherhood, remember that your worth is rooted in God's unchanging love, not in your accomplishments or challenges.

DAILY REFLECTION

What does it mean for you to feel truly rooted in God's love amidst the daily challenges of motherhood and life? How can you identify and nurture that love in your day-to-day experiences?

PRAYER

Dear God, thank you for surrounding me with your love and grace. Help me to anchor my heart in you, so that I may share that love with my family and those around me.

Rooted in God's love, we thrive even in the stormy seasons of life.

May 10

A Quiet Spirit, A Powerful Faith

"Rather, it should be that of your inner self, the unfading beauty of a gentle and quiet spirit, which is of great worth in God's sight." **1 Peter 3:4**

DEVOTIONAL

Cultivating a quiet spirit amidst life's storms can transform our faith into a powerful source of strength.

DAILY REFLECTION

What does it mean for you to cultivate a quiet spirit amidst the bustling demands of motherhood and life? How can you intentionally seek moments of peace to nourish your faith?

PRAYER

Heavenly Father, thank You for the strength You provide in the midst of our busy lives. Help us find serenity in our hearts and a deep faith that empowers us in our daily roles as mothers and women. Amen.

A truly quiet spirit holds the strength of the most powerful faith.

May 11

Mothering with Grace

"She opens her mouth with wisdom, and the teaching of kindness is on her tongue." **Proverbs 31:26**

DEVOTIONAL

Embrace each opportunity to respond with grace, understanding that this gentle approach creates lasting bonds with your children.

DAILY REFLECTION

What does it mean for you to mother with grace during the challenging moments of parenting? How can you invite God's strength into your responses today?

PRAYER

Dear Lord, thank You for the beautiful yet complex journey of motherhood. Please fill my heart with Your grace and patience as I nurture my children, guiding them with love.

Grace in motherhood is not the absence of struggle, but the presence of God in our hearts amidst it.

May 12

Persevering in Prayer

"Rejoice in hope, be patient in tribulation, be constant in prayer." **Romans 12:12**

DEVOTIONAL

In the midst of life's storms, remember that your perseverance in prayer strengthens your spirit and shapes your journey.

DAILY REFLECTION

What areas in your life feel heavy or unyielding right now, and how can you invite God into those moments through prayer?

PRAYER

Dear God, thank you for always being present in our lives. Help me to trust in Your timing and to keep my heart open as I persevere in prayer, knowing You hear me.

Persistent prayer cultivates patience and opens doors we couldn't imagine.

May 13

The Lord Is Your Shepherd

"The Lord is my shepherd; I shall not want. He makes me lie down in green pastures. He leads me beside still waters. He restores my soul."
Psalm 23:1-3

DEVOTIONAL

In the embrace of His care, trust that it's okay to step back and refuel, for the Lord watches over your heart and provides the peace your spirit longs for.

DAILY REFLECTION

What does it mean for you to trust that the Lord is guiding you, especially in the midst of your daily responsibilities as a mother and a woman of faith?

PRAYER

Dear Lord, thank You for being our Shepherd, guiding us with Your loving care. Help us to lean on You in times of uncertainty and to trust in Your path for our lives.

*Even in the busyness of life.
His guidance is always available to those who seek it.*

May 14

Letting Go of Bitterness

"See to it that no one falls short of the grace of God and that no bitter root grows up to cause trouble and defile many." **Hebrews 12:15**

DEVOTIONAL

Letting go of bitterness is an act of freedom that opens your heart to the joy and love waiting to embrace you.

DAILY REFLECTION

What bitterness or unresolved hurt are you carrying that might be weighing you down? How can you begin the process of letting that go today?

PRAYER

Dear Lord, help me to release the bitterness in my heart and embrace the freedom that forgiveness brings. Grant me the strength to let go of past hurts and the grace to heal.

*Bitterness is like drinking poison
and expecting the other person to suffer.*

May 15

Walking in Spiritual Freedom

"It is for freedom that Christ has set us free. Stand firm, then, and do not let yourselves be burdened again by a yoke of slavery." **Galatians 5:1**

DEVOTIONAL

Embrace the freedom that comes from letting go of what no longer serves you, and trust that you are designed for joy and purpose.

DAILY REFLECTION

What are the burdens you've been carrying that you need to lay down in order to walk more freely in your spiritual life? Consider the emotions and thoughts that may be holding you back from experiencing true freedom.

PRAYER

Dear God, thank you for the promise of freedom in You. Help me to release my burdens and trust in Your loving guidance as I walk through each day. Grant me the strength to embrace the spiritual journey ahead.

Freedom comes when we choose to let go of what weighs us down.

May 16

Your Story Isn't Over

"In their hearts humans plan their course, but the Lord establishes their steps." **Proverbs 16:9**

DEVOTIONAL

Your life is a tapestry still in the making, and every thread matters, no matter how frayed or vibrant it seems today.

DAILY REFLECTION

What dreams have been sidelined in your life, and how might God be inviting you to rekindle them today?

PRAYER

Dear God, thank you for the stories we each carry within us. Help me to see your hand in my life's journey, reminding me that it isn't over yet.

*Every chapter has its own beauty.
and every ending is but a new beginning.*

May 17

Strength to Forgive

"Be kind to one another, tenderhearted, forgiving one another, as God in Christ forgave you." **Ephesians 4:32**

DEVOTIONAL

Forgiveness is a gift we give ourselves, freeing our hearts and guiding us toward joy.

DAILY REFLECTION

What is one situation in your life where holding onto resentment has weighed you down, and how might choosing forgiveness lighten your heart?

PRAYER

Dear God, help me to release the burdens of anger and hurt. Grant me the strength to forgive those who have wronged me, and fill my heart with Your peace.

Forgiveness is not just an act of mercy; it's a gift we give ourselves.

May 18

Faithful Through the Seasons

"Your faithfulness endures to all generations; you have established the earth, and it stands fast." **Psalm 119:90**

DEVOTIONAL

Seasons may change, but God's unwavering faithfulness will always guide your journey through motherhood and beyond.

DAILY REFLECTION

What seasons of your life have challenged your faith the most, and how have you seen God's hand guiding you through them?

PRAYER

Gracious God, thank you for your unfailing presence in every season of our lives. Help me to trust you more deeply as I navigate the joys and struggles of motherhood and womanhood.

Even in the heaviest storms, God provides a shelter of peace.

May 19

Chosen and Cherished

"See, I have engraved you on the palms of my hands; your walls are ever before me." **Isaiah 49:16**

DEVOTIONAL

You are chosen for a purpose, and you are cherished not for what you do, but simply for who you are.

DAILY REFLECTION

What does it mean for you to feel chosen and cherished in your everyday life, and how can you actively remind yourself of this truth today?

PRAYER

Heavenly Father, thank You for reminding us that we are chosen and cherished in Your eyes. Help us to embrace our worth and share that love with those around us. May we find comfort in knowing we are never alone.

You are not just a mother;
you are a beloved daughter in the eyes of God.

May 20

God's Peace in Pressure

"Finally, brothers and sisters, whatever is true, whatever is noble, whatever is right, whatever is pure, whatever is lovely, whatever is admirable—if anything is excellent or praiseworthy—think about such things."
Philippians 4:8

DEVOTIONAL

In the midst of our busy lives, making space for God's peace can transform our pressure into purpose.

DAILY REFLECTION

What pressures are you facing right now that leave you feeling overwhelmed? How can you invite God into those situations to experience His peace?

PRAYER

Dear Lord, thank You for being our source of peace amidst life's chaos. Help us to lay our burdens at Your feet and trust in Your comforting presence today. Amen.

True peace is not found in the absence of pressure,
but in the presence of God.

May 21

A Life That Bears Fruit

"I will sing for the one I love a song about his vineyard: My loved one had a vineyard on a fertile hillside. He dug it up and cleared it of stones and planted it with the choicest vines; he built a watchtower in it and cut out a winepress as well. Then he looked for a crop of good grapes, but it yielded only bad fruit." **Isaiah 5:1-2**

DEVOTIONAL

Trust that your caring efforts are not in vain, for the seeds of love and wisdom you plant today may blossom into beautiful outcomes in the future.

DAILY REFLECTION

What does it mean for you to bear fruit in your everyday life, and how can you cultivate the seeds of purpose that God has planted in your heart?

PRAYER

Dear Lord, help me to embrace the beauty of the life you've given me. May I grow in faith, love, and service, bearing fruit that brings joy to my family and community. Amen.

Your life is a garden: cultivate it with love, patience, and purpose to yield the sweetest fruit.

May 22

Unshakeable Faith

"Though the mountains be shaken and the hills be removed, yet my unfailing love for you will not be shaken." **Isaiah 54:10**

DEVOTIONAL

Even in the face of storms, remember that God's love can be your anchor, keeping you grounded and steadfast.

DAILY REFLECTION

What are the storms in your life that challenge your faith, and how can you lean into God's promises during these times? Take a moment to reflect on His faithfulness in your past.

PRAYER

Dear Heavenly Father, help me to find strength in Your unwavering love. As I navigate the challenges of life, may my faith in You remain unshakeable, guiding my journey and illuminating my path.

In every challenge, faith is the anchor that holds us steady.

May 23

Celebrating Small Victories

"Therefore, since we are surrounded by such a great cloud of witnesses, let us throw off everything that hinders and the sin that so easily entangles. And let us run with perseverance the race marked out for us."
Hebrews 12:1

DEVOTIONAL

Sometimes, we need to remember that it's in the small, often unnoticed victories that we find strength and joy in our journey.

DAILY REFLECTION

What small victories have you experienced lately that brought a smile to your face or a sense of accomplishment to your heart? How can you take a moment to celebrate these wins today, no matter how minor they may seem?

PRAYER

Dear God, thank You for the small victories that fill our days with joy and gratitude. Help us to recognize and celebrate these moments, knowing that each one brings us closer to You and our true selves.

Every small victory is a step toward becoming the woman you're meant to be.

May 24

Serving with a Joyful Heart

"Whatever you do, work heartily, as for the Lord and not for men, knowing that from the Lord you will receive the inheritance as your reward."
Colossians 3:23-24

DEVOTIONAL

When you serve with joy, you not only bless others but also discover precious moments of connection within your own heart and home.

DAILY REFLECTION

What are some ways you can serve those around you this week that will bring you joy, rather than feeling like a burden?

PRAYER

Dear Lord, help me to serve with a joyful heart. May I find delight in my contributions and strive to reflect your love through my actions.

Serving others is not just an act: it's a blessing that flows back to us in unexpected ways.

May 25

When God Redirects Your Path

"Your word is a lamp to my feet and a light to my path."
Psalm 119:105

DEVOTIONAL

When God changes your course, trust that He has a beautiful purpose awaiting you, even if it isn't what you initially imagined.

DAILY REFLECTION

What unexpected change or detour in your life has brought about growth or new opportunities? How did that shift strengthen your faith or help you see God's hand at work?

PRAYER

Dear God, thank You for guiding my path, even when it doesn't go as planned. Help me to trust in Your divine redirection and embrace the new opportunities You place in my way.

*Sometimes the most beautiful journeys
are the ones we never intended to take.*

May 26

Healed and Whole in Christ

"For you died, and your life is now hidden with Christ in God. When Christ, who is your life, appears, then you also will appear with him in glory."
Colossians 3:3–4

DEVOTIONAL

You are not defined by your struggles or weariness; in Christ, you are renewed and made whole every day.

DAILY REFLECTION

What does it mean for you to feel healed and whole in Christ during this season of your life? How can you embrace His love and grace in your journey as a mother and woman?

PRAYER

Dear Lord, thank You for the promise of healing and wholeness in You. Help me to embrace Your love as I navigate the joys and challenges of life, and may I find peace in the knowledge that I am complete through Christ.

*You are not your past:
you are defined by His love and purpose for your future.*

May 27

The Joy of Obedience

"Delight yourself in the Lord, and He will give you the desires of your heart."
Psalm 37:4

DEVOTIONAL

Embracing obedience opens the door to joy and peace, inviting you to nurture your heart and spirit amidst the chaos of life.

DAILY REFLECTION

What areas of your life is God inviting you to embrace with joyful obedience, and how might that change your perspective today?

PRAYER

Dear Lord, thank You for the gift of obedience and the joy it brings when we walk in Your ways. Help me to embrace Your guidance with an open heart and trust in Your loving plans for my life.

Joy blossoms in the garden of obedience,
where trust takes root and faith flourishes.

May 28

Courage to Trust Again

"But blessed is the one who trusts in the Lord, whose confidence is in him. They will be like a tree planted by the water that sends out its roots by the stream. It does not fear when heat comes; its leaves are always green. It has no worries in a year of drought and never fails to bear fruit."
Jeremiah 17:7-8

DEVOTIONAL

Trusting again requires courage, but through small, intentional steps of faith, you can open your heart to the beauty of connection.

DAILY REFLECTION

What experiences have made it difficult for you to trust again? Can you imagine how life might look if you chose to step forward in faith?

PRAYER

Dear God, grant her the courage to open her heart again, to release the weight of past pain, and to step into each new day with hope and trust. Surround her with your love and remind her that she is never alone.

Trust is a bridge built from the heart,
and it can be rebuilt one brave step at a time.

May 29

Restoring What Was Lost

"Restore us to yourself, O Lord, that we may be restored; renew our days as of old." **Lamentations 5:21**

DEVOTIONAL

Even in the busyness of life, you can actively seek to restore what was lost by creating new memories and nurturing relationships that bring joy.

DAILY REFLECTION

What areas of your life feel like they could use restoration, and how might you invite God into those spaces?

PRAYER

Dear Heavenly Father, I come to You with a heart that longs for restoration. Please help me to recognize the beauty in what was lost and guide me as I seek healing and renewal.

Restoration begins when we allow ourselves to embrace the beauty of letting go and making room for new beginnings.

May 30

Finishing the Month Faithfully

"When you pass through the waters, I will be with you; and when you pass through the rivers, they will not sweep over you. When you walk through the fire, you will not be burned; the flames will not set you ablaze."
Isaiah 43:2

DEVOTIONAL

Embrace each day as an opportunity to cultivate connection rather than perfection.

DAILY REFLECTION

What are some ways you can intentionally close this month in gratitude and faith, reflecting on both your challenges and your victories?

PRAYER

Dear God, as this month comes to a close, help me to see Your hand in my life and to finish it with a heart full of gratitude. Amen.

Faithfully embracing the end of a season allows for a beautiful new beginning.

May 31

Faith That Perseveres

"For you have need of endurance, so that after you have done the will of God, you may receive the promise."
Hebrews 10:36

DEVOTIONAL

Embrace your journey with faith, knowing that perseverance today shapes the beautiful promise of tomorrow.

DAILY REFLECTION

What challenges in your life require a perseverance rooted in faith? How can you lean into God's promise during these times?

PRAYER

Dear Lord, grant me the strength to persevere through life's challenges, embracing faith as my foundation. Help me to trust in Your goodness and to find hope even in the smallest moments.

Faith isn't just about believing: it's the strength to keep moving forward when the path seems unclear.

June 1

God's Timing Is Always Right

"When the time is right, I, the Lord, will make it happen."
Isaiah 60:22

DEVOTIONAL

God's timing can feel like a mystery, but trust that He knows when and how to reveal His plans for you.

DAILY REFLECTION

What areas of your life are you waiting for God to move? How can you trust Him more deeply in this season of waiting?

PRAYER

Dear God, thank you for Your perfect timing in every season of our lives. Help me to trust in Your plans and rest in the assurance that You are always at work, even when I can't see it.

God's timing is a tapestry woven
with threads of grace, purpose, and love.

June 2

Living with Open Hands

"Open your mouth wide, and I will fill it, says the Lord." **Psalm 81:10**

DEVOTIONAL

In this season of life, filled with various responsibilities and roles, remember that openness invites blessings. When we release our tight grip on control and expectations, we allow God to fill us with joy, peace, and unexpected moments of beauty.

DAILY REFLECTION

What does it mean for you to live with open hands, inviting both gifting and letting go in your daily life? How might this practice transform your relationship with your family and your own sense of purpose?

PRAYER

Lord, help me to embrace life with open hands. Teach me to receive your blessings gratefully and to release my worries and fears into your care. May I find joy in the gift of each moment.

Living with open hands unlocks
the blessings of both giving and receiving.

June 3

The Power of God's Word

"For the word of God is alive and active. Sharper than any double-edged sword, it penetrates even to dividing soul and spirit, joints and marrow; it judges the thoughts and attitudes of the heart." **Hebrews 4:12**

DEVOTIONAL

The ability to nourish our spirits through God's Word allows us to approach life's challenges with renewed perspective and strength.

DAILY REFLECTION

What words are you holding on to today that speak life into your circumstances, and how can you lean more into God's promises to guide you?

PRAYER

Dear Heavenly Father, thank You for the gift of Your Word, a beacon of truth in our lives. Help me to lean on its promises and find strength in its wisdom as I navigate my days.

God's Word is a balm for the weary soul,
offering peace and clarity amidst life's storms.

June 4

Anchored in Hope

"Praise be to the God and Father of our Lord Jesus Christ! In his great mercy he has given us new birth into a living hope through the resurrection of Jesus Christ from the dead, and into an inheritance that can never perish, spoil or fade. This inheritance is kept in heaven for you,..."
1 Peter 1:3-4

DEVOTIONAL

In the midst of life's challenges, remember that your hope in Christ is like an anchor, steadying you as you navigate the waters of motherhood and daily life.

DAILY REFLECTION

What anchors your hope in this season of life, and how can you draw strength from those anchors as you navigate your daily challenges?

PRAYER

Dear God, thank you for being our steadfast anchor in times of uncertainty. Help me to feel your presence each day and strengthen my hope in you, knowing that you hold all things together.

Hope is the lighthouse that guides us through the storms of life.

June 5

Trusting God's Process

"Trust in the Lord and do good; dwell in the land and enjoy safe pasture. Take delight in the Lord, and he will give you the desires of your heart. Commit your way to the Lord; trust in him and he will do this."
Psalm 37:3-5

DEVOTIONAL

Trusting God's process means surrendering our need to control the timeline of our lives, allowing us to find peace even amidst the messiness of motherhood.

DAILY REFLECTION

What areas of your life feel uncertain right now, and how can you invite God into those situations where you're struggling to trust His process?

PRAYER

Dear God, thank you for your unwavering presence in our lives. Help me to surrender my worries and fully trust in your perfect timing and plan. Amen.

Growth often comes in the quiet moments where we lean into the unknown and embrace the journey.

June 6

Purpose in the Pain

*"Therefore we do not lose heart. Though outwardly we are wasting away, yet inwardly we are being renewed day by day. For our light and momentary troubles are achieving for us an eternal glory that far outweighs them all. So we fix our eyes not on what is seen, but on what is unseen, since what is seen is temporary, but what is unseen is eternal." **2 Corinthians 4:16-18***

DEVOTIONAL

Embrace the truth that your pain can serve a purpose, leading to growth and beauty that you may not yet see.

DAILY REFLECTION

What are some of the painful experiences in your life that have shaped you and led you to discover deeper aspects of yourself? How might these experiences be guiding you toward your true purpose?

PRAYER

Dear God, thank you for being with us in our moments of pain. Help us to see the glimmers of hope and purpose that arise from our struggles, and guide us as we grow through them.

In every season of pain, there blooms a purpose that can only be realized through our struggles.

June 7

Finding Rest in Surrender

"Therefore, I urge you, sisters, in view of God's mercy, to offer your bodies as living sacrifices, holy and pleasing to God—this is your true and proper worship. Do not conform to the pattern of this world, but be transformed by the renewing of your mind." **Romans 12:1-2**

DEVOTIONAL

When you surrender your worries to God, you create a pathway for peace to flow into your life.

DAILY REFLECTION

What does surrendering to God in your daily life look like, and how can you embrace it as a source of rest amidst your responsibilities?

PRAYER

Dear God, help me to release my burdens into Your hands. Grant me the peace that comes from trusting You fully and enable me to find solace in surrender.

Surrender is not giving up; it's opening your heart to a greater plan.

June 8

Spiritual Refreshment

"O God, you are my God; earnestly I seek you; my soul thirsts for you, my whole body longs for you, in a dry and weary land where there is no water." **Psalm 63:1**

DEVOTIONAL

Even on the busiest days, taking time to seek spiritual refreshment can rejuvenate your spirit and renew your strength.

DAILY REFLECTION

What activities or moments in your life truly refresh your spirit, and how can you incorporate more of them into your daily routine?

PRAYER

Dear God, thank you for the gift of this day. Please help me to seek moments of spiritual refreshment, allowing my heart to be renewed in Your presence.

Amid the busyness of life, a refreshed spirit can bloom in stillness.

June 9

A New Song in Your Heart

"Sing to the Lord a new song, for he has done marvelous things; his right hand and his holy arm have worked salvation for him." **Psalm 98:1**

DEVOTIONAL

Embrace the changes in your life as an opportunity to create a new melody, for every season carries the potential for a beautiful transformation.

DAILY REFLECTION

What new melody is God inviting you to sing in this season of your life? How can you tune your heart to His voice amidst the routine of motherhood and daily responsibilities?

PRAYER

Dear Lord, thank You for the gift of a new day and a new song to sing. Help me listen for Your voice and embrace the fresh melodies You place in my heart, no matter how small.

Every new season births a new song:
let your spirit dance to its rhythm.

June 10

Confident in His Calling

"Be confident in the calling you have received, knowing that you are beautifully and wonderfully made for this purpose." **Ephesians 4:1**

DEVOTIONAL

Embrace your unique calling with confidence, for every season of your life adds depth and meaning to your journey.

DAILY REFLECTION

What doubts or fears arise in your heart when you think about the calling God has placed in your life, and how can you embrace His confidence today?

PRAYER

Dear Lord, thank you for the unique calling you have placed on my life. Help me to embrace that calling with confidence, trusting in Your guidance and strength each day.

Your calling is not just a destination:
it's a journey of purpose woven through each moment of your life.

June 11

Healing Takes Time

*"Yet the Lord longs to be gracious to you; therefore he will rise up to show you compassion. For the Lord is a God of justice. Blessed are all who wait for him!" **Isaiah 30:18***

DEVOTIONAL

Healing is a journey marked by patience, reminding you that each day is a step toward wholeness.

DAILY REFLECTION

What parts of your life feel in need of healing right now, and how can you allow yourself the grace of time in this process?

PRAYER

Dear God, thank you for your steady presence in our lives as we navigate healing. Help us to embrace the journey, knowing that each step is part of your perfect plan.

*Healing is not a destination,
but a gentle path that unfolds with patience and love.*

June 12

Peace When You Don't Understand

*"You will keep in perfect peace those whose minds are steadfast, because they trust in you." **Isaiah 26:3***

DEVOTIONAL

Even when circumstances feel beyond our understanding, we can find peace by trusting in God's perfect plan for our lives and our families.

DAILY REFLECTION

What situations in your life currently feel overwhelming or confusing, and how might you seek peace in those moments of uncertainty?

PRAYER

Dear Lord, grant me the peace that surpasses understanding as I navigate the complexities of life. Help me to trust in Your divine plan, even when I can't see the way forward.

In the midst of chaos, the heart can find a quiet place of refuge.

June 13

Your Prayers Matter

"Call to me and I will answer you and tell you great and unsearchable things you do not know." **Jeremiah 33:3**

DEVOTIONAL

Your prayers, however simple or desperate, are powerful tools that shape not just your life but the lives of those you love.

DAILY REFLECTION

What worries or hopes have you been holding in your heart lately? How can you invite God into those moments through prayer?

PRAYER

Dear Lord, thank you for listening to my heart and for the assurance that my prayers matter. Help me to lean into Your presence and trust in Your perfect timing.

Every whispered prayer is a seed planted in faith, waiting for God's garden to bloom.

June 14

When God Feels Distant

"So do not fear, for I am with you; do not be dismayed, for I am your God. I will strengthen you and help you; I will uphold you with my righteous right hand." **Isaiah 41:10**

DEVOTIONAL

In the moments when God feels distant, remember that His presence may be felt in the quiet whispers of reflections from your past, guiding you back home.

DAILY REFLECTION

What moments in your life make you feel as though God is far away? How can you invite Him into those feelings and situations today?

PRAYER

Dear God, thank you for always being present, even when I struggle to feel Your closeness. Help me to remember that You are always near, even in the silence.

Even in the quiet spaces, God is crafting a deeper relationship with us.

June 15

His Mercy is Enough

*"But because of His great love for us, God, who is rich in mercy, made us alive with Christ even when we were dead in transgressions—it is by grace you have been saved." **Ephesians 2:4-5***

DEVOTIONAL

You are enough, not because of what you achieve, but because His mercy blankets you in every moment of uncertainty and imperfection.

DAILY REFLECTION

What areas of your life do you find yourself striving for perfection, and how might you extend grace to yourself in those moments?

PRAYER

Dear Lord, thank you for the boundless mercy You show us daily. Help me to embrace Your grace and remember that at my weakest, Your mercy is more than enough.

His mercy meets us in our messiness and transforms our struggles into stories of hope.

June 16

Walking Boldly with God

"May the God of hope fill you with all joy and peace as you trust in Him."
Romans 15:13

DEVOTIONAL

Boldness comes when we step out of our fears and into faith, remembering that God is always with us, guiding both our paths and those we love.

DAILY REFLECTION

What does it mean for you to walk boldly with God in your everyday life, and where is He inviting you to step forward in faith today?

PRAYER

Dear God, help me to embrace the courage you offer me each day. May I feel your presence guiding me as I navigate my roles as a mother and a woman of faith. Give me the strength to trust in you, knowing that with every step, I'm never alone.

Boldly stepping forward often leads to the most beautiful experiences.

June 17

Less of Me, More of Him

"He must increase, but I must decrease."
John 3:30

DEVOTIONAL

Sometimes, remembering to step back and invite God in allows us to experience the freedom we desperately seek.

DAILY REFLECTION

What does it look like in your daily life to prioritize God's presence over your own concerns and desires? How can you cultivate deeper reliance on Him as you navigate motherhood and the challenges of everyday life?

PRAYER

Dear Lord, help me to set aside my worries and desires, allowing Your light to shine through me. Teach me to embrace less of my own agenda and more of Your divine purpose each day.

To find our true selves, we must first lose ourselves in Him.

June 18

The Joy of Trusting

"Commit to the LORD whatever you do, and he will establish your plans."
Proverbs 16:3

DEVOTIONAL

Trusting God is not about having all the answers but finding joy and peace in His perfect plan as you embrace each day with faith and love.

DAILY REFLECTION

What does trusting God with your daily worries and responsibilities look like for you in this season of your life?

PRAYER

Dear Lord, help me to lay my fears and anxieties at Your feet. Grant me the strength to trust in Your perfect plan for my life and my family.

Trusting gives your heart the freedom to dance in the midst of uncertainty.

June 19

A Light for the World

"When Jesus spoke again to the people, he said, 'I am the light of the world. Whoever follows me will never walk in darkness but will have the light of life.'" **John 8:12**

DEVOTIONAL

Remember that your light can shine brightly in the simplest moments of parenting, showing the world the beauty of grace and love.

DAILY REFLECTION

What does it mean for you to be a light in the lives of those around you, especially your family and friends? How can you intentionally shine God's love in your everyday moments?

PRAYER

Dear God, thank You for the gift of light that You have placed within us. Help me to shine brightly in my home and community, reflecting Your love and grace to those I encounter each day.

Your light not only brightens your path but also illuminates the way for others.

June 20

Spirit-Led Living

"If we live by the Spirit, let us also keep in step with the Spirit."
Galatians 5:25

DEVOTIONAL

The takeaway for you, dear woman, is this: Embrace the moments of stillness and listen for the Spirit's leading, for in those moments lies the power to enrich both your life and the lives of others around you.

DAILY REFLECTION

What does it look like for you to surrender control and trust the Holy Spirit in your daily decisions and interactions?

PRAYER

Dear God, help me to embrace the gentle leading of Your Spirit in my life. Teach me to listen closely and respond faithfully to Your guidance, finding peace in surrender.

Spirit-led living is not about knowing every step ahead, but about trusting in the One who walks beside us.

June 21

He Sees Every Tear

"You keep track of all my sorrows. You have collected all my tears in your bottle. You have recorded each one in your book." **Psalm 56:8**

DEVOTIONAL

Each tear you shed is noted and cherished by God teaching you that your feelings matter.

DAILY REFLECTION

What tearful moments have shaped your journey, and how can you invite God into those sacred spaces?

PRAYER

Dear God, thank you for seeing every tear that falls and for holding each moment close to your heart. Help me to remember that I am never alone in my struggles, and guide me to find comfort in your presence.

Every tear you shed is a testament to your strength and a mark of His eternal love.

June 22

The Beauty of Dependence

"Those who know your name will trust in you, for you, Lord, have never forsaken those who seek you." **Psalm 9:10**

DEVOTIONAL

When you allow yourself to depend on God, you invite His strength into your life, creating room for His grace to transform your challenges into opportunities for growth.

DAILY REFLECTION

What does it mean for you to rely on God in your everyday life, and how might that dependency bring you a sense of peace and strength?

PRAYER

Dear Lord, thank You for inviting us into a relationship of trust and dependence with You. Help us to embrace Your guidance and love, finding strength in our vulnerabilities as we journey through life. Amen.

True strength often lies in the grace to lean on the One who knows us best.

June 23

A Life of Overflow

"The thief comes only to steal and kill and destroy; I have come that they may have life, and have it to the full." **John 10:10**

DEVOTIONAL

Remember that your life is meant to be an overflow of joy and purpose, even amid the everyday challenges; seek out and cherish the blessings that fill your heart.

DAILY REFLECTION

What does living a life of overflow look like for you in your daily routines as a mom, professional, and friend? How can you cultivate abundance in your heart and share it with those around you?

PRAYER

Dear God, thank you for the blessings you pour into our lives each day. Help me to recognize the overflow of your love and grace, sharing it generously with my family and community.

From the abundance of your heart, your actions will flow.

June 24

The Lord Will Provide

"So Abraham called that place The Lord Will Provide; and to this day it is said, 'On the mountain of the Lord it will be provided.'" **Genesis 22:14**

DEVOTIONAL

When we relinquish our fears and trust in God's provision, we often discover solutions that surpass our expectations.

DAILY REFLECTION

What areas of your life do you find yourself doubting God's provision, and how might you shift your perspective to trust Him more fully?

PRAYER

Dear Lord, thank You for Your constant provision in our lives. Help us to trust in Your timing and to recognize the blessings You give us each day.

Faith opens the door to abundance, often in ways we never expected.

June 25

Standing in Spiritual Authority

"No, in all these things we are more than conquerors through him who loved us." **Romans 8:37**

DEVOTIONAL

We possess an innate resilience and strength, empowered by our faith, to make choices that honor both our families and ourselves.

DAILY REFLECTION

What does it mean for you to stand firm in your spiritual authority, and how can you exercise it in your daily life as a mother and a woman of faith?

PRAYER

Heavenly Father, thank You for the gift of Your strength and guidance. Help me to embrace my spiritual authority with confidence and grace as I navigate the challenges of each day. Fill me with Your peace and courage to lead myself and my family in Your truth.

Embracing my spiritual authority empowers not just me, but those I love.

June 26

Faith Over Frustration

"Cast all your anxiety on him because he cares for you."
1 Peter 5:7

DEVOTIONAL

When frustration rises, remember to pause, breathe, and cast your cares on Him, for peace can be your choice even in chaos.

DAILY REFLECTION

What are the frustrations in your life right now that challenge your faith, and how might embracing faith shift your perspective on them?

PRAYER

Dear God, help me to surrender my frustrations to You. Fill my heart with Your peace and guide me to trust in Your plan, even when things feel overwhelming.

Faith doesn't eliminate the frustration: it helps us rise above it.

June 27

Renewed by Grace

"But he gives us more grace. That is why Scripture says: 'God opposes the proud but shows favor to the humble.'" **James 4:6**

DEVOTIONAL

Embrace the grace that renews you daily; it's in your vulnerability and acceptance that true strength and beauty emerge.

DAILY REFLECTION

What does it mean for you to embrace grace in these busy, beautiful years of motherhood? How can you allow that grace to renew your spirit today?

PRAYER

Dear Lord, thank you for the gift of Your grace that flows endlessly into our lives. Help me to open my heart to receive it fully, so I may reflect Your love in my family and my everyday moments.

Grace whispers hope into the weary heart, reminding us that we are always loved, always renewed.

June 28

The Gift of His Presence

"The Lord is near to all who call on Him, to all who call on Him in truth." **Psalm 145:18**

DEVOTIONAL

Embrace the quiet moments, for they are often where you can feel His presence the strongest.

DAILY REFLECTION

What does it mean to you, in the midst of your busy life as a mom, to intentionally seek the presence of God each day? How does recognizing His constant companionship change your perspective on the challenges you face?

PRAYER

Heavenly Father, thank You for the gift of Your presence in our lives. Help us to slow down and be aware of You around us, finding comfort and strength in Your love today.

In the stillness, we find Him waiting, ready to embrace us with peace.

June 29

Finish Strong in Faith

, "Now may the God of peace, who brought up our Lord Jesus from the dead, equip you with all you need for doing his will May he produce in you, through the power of the Spirit, all that is pleasing to him. All glory to him forever and ever! Amen." **Hebrews 13:20-21**

DEVOTIONAL

Finish strong by trusting that God not only walks beside you but also fully equips you to thrive in every season of life.

DAILY REFLECTION

What does it mean for you to finish strong in your faith as you navigate the many roles you play in life? How can you draw closer to God in this season and trust Him to guide you through challenges?

PRAYER

Dear God, thank you for being our steadfast support and guide. Help me deepen my faith as I embrace this journey ahead and strengthen my resolve to finish strong, knowing You are with me every step of the way.

Faith is not just a destination;
it's a journey we embrace until the very end.

June 30

Freedom in Christ

"Live as free people, but do not use your freedom as a cover-up for evil; live as God's servants." **1 Peter 2:16**

DEVOTIONAL

Embracing freedom in Christ means letting go of self-imposed limitations and trusting that your worth is inherent, not earned through perfection or productivity.

DAILY REFLECTION

What areas of your life do you feel weighed down by expectations, and how can you invite Christ's freedom into those spaces today?

PRAYER

Dear Lord, thank you for the gift of freedom that comes through our relationship with You. Help me to embrace this freedom daily and to release the burdens that hold me back.

In Christ, we shed the weight of the world's expectations
and rise with the lightness of His grace.

Halfway Through Our Journey

You are now halfway through this devotional journey.

Many women discover this book through the thoughtful reviews shared by readers like you.

If these pages have supported your faith and daily reflection, would you consider sharing a short review on Amazon?

Your voice may help someone else find encouragement today.

devo.anchoredgraces.com/2026

July 1

God's Love Never Fails

"Give thanks to the Lord, for he is good; his love endures forever."
Psalm 136:1

DEVOTIONAL

No matter how overwhelming life feels, remember that God's love is unfailing and always brings us back to what truly matters.

DAILY REFLECTION

What are the moments in your life when you've felt most overwhelmed, and how can you remind yourself of God's unwavering love in those times?

PRAYER

Dear God, thank you for your constant presence in our lives. Help us to feel your love surrounding us, especially in our moments of doubt and fear. May we always find comfort in the promise that your love never fails.

Even in the storms, God's love is the anchor for our souls.

July 2

Courage to Follow God's Call

"I will instruct you and teach you in the way you should go; I will counsel you with my loving eye on you." **Psalm 32:8**

DEVOTIONAL

Embrace the whispers of your heart; they might be the divine calling inviting you to step into your true purpose.

DAILY REFLECTION

What does it mean for you to have the courage to follow God's call in your life, and what steps might you take today to embrace that path?

PRAYER

Dear God, grant me the courage to listen and respond to Your call. Help me to trust in Your guidance as I navigate the path You've set before me. May I find strength in each step I take, knowing that I am never alone.

*Your journey of faith is uniquely yours,
and it blooms beautifully when nurtured with courage.*

July 3

True Freedom Through Faith

"Now the Lord is the Spirit, and where the Spirit of the Lord is, there is freedom." **2 Corinthians 3:17**

DEVOTIONAL

True freedom comes not from a life free of challenges, but from trusting in God amidst those challenges.

DAILY REFLECTION

What does true freedom look like in your life, and how does your faith guide you toward it each day? Reflect on the moments when you've felt liberated in your spirit and the ways you can nurture that freedom further.

PRAYER

Dear Lord, help me to embrace the freedom that comes from trusting in You. Teach me to let go of burdens that weigh me down and to walk in the light of Your love each day. Amen.

True freedom is found not in the absence of trials, but in the presence of faith.

July 4

Faith in the Everyday

"Taste and see that the Lord is good; blessed is the one who takes refuge in him." **Psalm 34:8**

DEVOTIONAL

Your faith is not just a belief; it's a discovery of God's presence that unfolds through the everyday gifts you often overlook.

DAILY REFLECTION

What small moments today can you invite God into, allowing faith to transform the ordinary into the extraordinary?

PRAYER

Dear God, thank you for being present in the everyday moments of my life. Help me to see your hand at work in both the small and significant things today.

Faith is not reserved for Sundays; it thrives in the rhythm of our daily lives.

July 5

Abiding in Peace

"Abide in me, and I in you. As the branch cannot bear fruit by itself, unless it abides in the vine, neither can you, unless you abide in me." **John 15:4**

DEVOTIONAL

Abiding in peace means consciously choosing to nurture your spirit, trusting that through every season, God's presence is your greatest source of strength.

DAILY REFLECTION

What does it look like for you to truly abide in peace amidst the busyness of motherhood and daily life? Can you identify moments where you feel His presence, calming your heart and guiding your thoughts?

PRAYER

Dear God, as I navigate the challenges of each day, help me to find your peace in every moment. Remind me that I can rest in you, letting go of worries and embracing your love. Thank you for your gentle presence.

Peace is not the absence of trouble, but the presence of Christ.

July 6

Living for an Audience of One

"You are precious in my eyes, and honored, and I love you." **Isaiah 43:4**

DEVOTIONAL

When we center our lives on God's love and approval, it transforms not just our perspective, but also our purpose, reminding us that we are enough just as we are.

DAILY REFLECTION

What does it look like for you to prioritize God's approval over the world's expectations in your daily life? How can you tune your heart to hear His voice amid the noise around you?

PRAYER

Dear Lord, help me to quiet the distractions of life and focus my heart solely on You. May I find my worth in Your love and guidance as I navigate my responsibilities and relationships each day.

Freedom comes when we embrace who we are in Him, not who the world wants us to be.

July 7

Finding Stillness with God

"Turn away from evil and do good; seek peace and pursue it."
Psalm 34:14

DEVOTIONAL

In the midst of life's demands, taking a moment to find stillness with God can rejuvenate your spirit and reaffirm your peace.

DAILY REFLECTION

What does finding stillness with God look like for you in the midst of your busy life as a mom and woman?

PRAYER

Dear God, help me to carve out moments in my day to simply be with You. Let Your peace wash over me and guide my thoughts as I seek stillness in Your presence.

In the quiet moments, our hearts can hear the gentle whispers of God.

July 8

The Strength of Surrender

"This is what the Sovereign Lord, the Holy One of Israel, says: 'In repentance and rest is your salvation, in quietness and trust is your strength."
Isaiah 30:15

DEVOTIONAL

Sometimes, the greatest strength comes from letting go and allowing God's grace to guide us.

DAILY REFLECTION

What does surrender mean for you in this season of your life, and how might embracing it lead to newfound strength and peace?

PRAYER

Dear God, help me to release my burdens and trust in Your plan. Grant me the courage to surrender my worries and find strength in Your presence every day.

True strength is found not in holding on tightly, \but in the quiet power of letting go.

July 9

Becoming a Woman of Influence

"Charm is deceptive, and beauty is fleeting; but a woman who fears the Lord is to be praised." **Proverbs 31:30**

DEVOTIONAL

Every small act of love and understanding you share has the power to shape the next generation.

DAILY REFLECTION

What does it mean for you to influence those around you? How can your unique experiences and insights shape the lives of others in your family, community, or circle of friends?

PRAYER

Dear God, thank you for the unique woman you've created me to be. Help me to recognize and embrace the influence I have, using it to uplift and inspire those around me.

Your influence is the quiet strength that can steer the hearts of many.

July 10

Trust When You Can't See

"It is the glory of God to conceal a matter; to search out a matter is the glory of kings." **Proverbs 25:2**

DEVOTIONAL

When trust feels challenging, remember that the journey of faith is about moving forward in hope, even in the face of uncertainty.

DAILY REFLECTION

What areas of your life do you find it hardest to trust God with when the path ahead is unclear?

PRAYER

Dear God, help me to embrace Your promises even when I can't see the way forward. Fill my heart with peace as I lean on Your understanding, trusting You to guide my steps.

Faith is not about seeing the path ahead; it's about trusting the One who already knows the way.

July 11

Grace That Covers All

"But He said to me, 'My grace is sufficient for you, for my power is made perfect in weakness.' Therefore I will boast all the more gladly of my weaknesses, so that the power of Christ may rest upon me."
2 Corinthians 12:9

DEVOTIONAL

Even in our moments of weakness and uncertainty, God's grace wraps around us, providing reassurance that we are enough just as we are.

DAILY REFLECTION

What areas of your life do you need to remind yourself that God's grace covers you completely, despite your imperfections and challenges?

PRAYER

Dear God, thank You for Your boundless grace that embraces us even when we feel unworthy. Help us to accept this grace in our lives and extend it to ourselves and others.

Grace is not only a gift; it is the soothing balm that heals our weary souls and reminds us we are loved just as we are.

July 12

Letting God Lead

"In their hearts, humans plan their course, but the Lord establishes their steps." **Proverbs 16:9**

DEVOTIONAL

There's profound freedom in surrendering your plans to God; it opens the door to His perfect guidance and allows you to embrace the beauty of His unfolding journey.

DAILY REFLECTION

What areas of your life are you holding onto tightly, and how might it feel to release those to God's guidance?

PRAYER

Dear God, help me to trust in Your plan and relinquish control over my worries. Lead me gently toward the paths You have already prepared for me.

Letting go of control opens the door for God to lead us toward something far greater than ourselves.

July 13

Rejoicing in Trials

"Consider it pure joy, my sisters, whenever you face trials of many kinds, because you know that the testing of your faith produces perseverance. Let perseverance finish its work so that you may be mature and complete, not lacking anything." **James 1:2-4**

DEVOTIONAL

The trials in our lives can serve as stepping stones towards greater faith and maturity, reminding us that we are more capable than we realize.

DAILY REFLECTION

What trials are you currently experiencing, and how can you see God's hand at work within those challenges? Take a moment to reflect on how these struggles might be shaping you for the better.

PRAYER

Dear God, thank you for being with me in my trials. Help me to find joy in every challenge and to trust that you are working for my good, even when the path feels uncertain.

Joy does not deny the pain: it rises above it, shining light on the hope that endures.

July 14

The Power of Spiritual Discipline

"I pray that out of his glorious riches he may strengthen you with power through his Spirit in your inner being, 17 so that Christ may dwell in your hearts through faith. And I pray that you, being rooted and established in love,..." **Ephesians 3:16-17**

DEVOTIONAL

Our spiritual discipline is the foundation that helps us navigate and find peace amidst life's chaos.

DAILY REFLECTION

What areas of your life could benefit from more intentional spiritual discipline, and how might that transform your days and relationships?

PRAYER

Dear God, thank You for being present in our daily lives. Help us embrace the routines that draw us closer to You, giving us grace to seek Your presence with purpose and joy.

Spiritual discipline is not a burden but a bridge to a deeper relationship with God.

July 15

Your Past Does Not Define You

"I praise you because I am fearfully and wonderfully made; your works are wonderful, I know that full well." **Psalm 139:14**

DEVOTIONAL

You are not the sum of your past experiences; you are a continually evolving masterpiece, crafted by the hands of love.

DAILY REFLECTION

What memories from your past do you find yourself clinging to, and how might you release them to embrace the woman you've become?

PRAYER

Dear God, help me to let go of the weight of my past and to see myself through Your loving eyes. Remind me daily that I am defined by Your grace and not by my mistakes.

Your past may shape your story, but it does not have the power to rewrite who you are destined to be.

July 16

Choosing Joy Over Anxiety

"Do not be anxious about anything, but in every situation, by prayer and petition, with thanksgiving, present your requests to God." **Philippians 4:6**

DEVOTIONAL

Choosing joy amidst the noise of life often requires a deliberate decision to focus on gratitude, intentionally inviting God's peace into our busy hearts.

DAILY REFLECTION

What are the moments in your day when anxiety creeps in, and how can you intentionally choose joy instead?

PRAYER

Dear God, thank you for the gift of today. Help me to embrace joy in the midst of worries and remind me of your presence in every moment.

Joy is a choice we make, an anchor in the storm of life's uncertainties.

July 17

Delight in the Lord

"The steps of a woman are established by the Lord, and when she falls, she will not be hurled headlong, because the Lord is the one who holds her hand." **Psalm 37:23-24**

DEVOTIONAL

Find joy in the small moments and trust that in the chaos of life, God's delight is found in your heart as you seek Him.

DAILY REFLECTION

What are the moments in your day where you feel a spark of joy that reminds you of God's presence in your life? How can you cultivate more of those moments, inviting delight into your daily routine?

PRAYER

Dear Lord, thank you for the joy you bring into our lives, often hidden in the ordinary. Help me to recognize and delight in your presence every day, nurturing a heart that seeks you.

Delighting in the Lord transforms the mundane into a meaningful journey.

July 18

Finding Balance in God's Design

"The Lord God said, 'It is not good for the man to be alone. I will make a helper suitable for him." **Genesis 2:18**

DEVOTIONAL

Finding balance isn't about doing it all, but rather about recognizing that God designed you to thrive in community, sharing burdens and joys with others.

DAILY REFLECTION

What areas of your life feel out of balance, and how can you invite God into those spaces to bring His design for harmony?

PRAYER

Dear Lord, help me to recognize the beauty in Your design and guide me as I seek balance in my life. May Your peace fill the areas where I feel overwhelmed, and help me to trust in Your perfect plan.

Balance is not something you find; it's something you create with God's guidance.

July 19

Hope in the Wilderness

"See, I am doing a new thing! Now it springs up; do you not perceive it? I am making a way in the wilderness and streams in the wasteland."
Isaiah 43:19

DEVOTIONAL

Amidst the challenges of life, hope often arises in the most unexpected places, reminding us that we can find beauty and growth in the wilderness.

DAILY REFLECTION

What wilderness experience are you facing right now, and how can you invite hope into that situation? Consider the ways you've seen God work in past challenges and how those memories can encourage you today.

PRAYER

Dear God, as I navigate this season of uncertainty, let Your presence be a constant reminder of hope. Help me to trust in Your plan and to see the beauty in the wilderness of my journey.

In the wilderness, hope is not lost; it blooms quietly, waiting for the right moment to reveal its beauty.

July 20

You Are God's Masterpiece

"For we are God's handiwork, created in Christ Jesus to do good works, which God prepared in advance for us to do." **Ephesians 2:10**

DEVOTIONAL

You are intricately designed and irreplaceably valued, so embrace the masterpiece you are becoming, knowing that your journey has purpose and beauty just as it is.

DAILY REFLECTION

What unique attributes do you possess that reflect God's creativity in your life? How can you honor those traits as part of your journey?

PRAYER

Dear Lord, thank You for creating me as Your masterpiece. Help me to see my worth in Your eyes and to embrace the beauty and purpose You have instilled in me.

Your imperfections are part of what makes you uniquely beautiful in the eyes of your Creator.

July 21

Living Loved and Known

"Because of the Lord's great love we are not consumed, for his compassions never fail. They are new every morning; great is your faithfulness." **Lamentations 3:22-23**

DEVOTIONAL

You are deeply loved and known by God, and His mercies are constantly renewing your spirit, enabling you to thrive in the beautiful mess of life.

DAILY REFLECTION

What does it feel like to truly embrace the fact that you are both loved and known by God? How can this understanding change the way you approach your daily life and interactions with others?

PRAYER

Dear God, thank You for loving me unconditionally and knowing me deeply. Help me to rest in this truth and to reflect Your love in all I do.

To be loved and known is the greatest gift, unlocking the door to authentic living.

July 22

The Voice That Calms

"You of little faith, why are you so afraid?"
Matthew 8:26

DEVOTIONAL

When life feels tumultuous, remember to pause and listen for that still, comforting voice that brings calm to the chaos.

DAILY REFLECTION

What voices do you allow to speak into your life, and how do they influence your peace and well-being?

PRAYER

Dear God, thank You for always being a calming presence in our lives. Help me to recognize and lean into Your voice amidst the chaos of daily life. Amen.

The quiet whisper of His love can calm the loudest storms within.

July 23

Returning to Your First Love

*"Yet I hold this against you: You have forsaken the love you had at first. Consider how far you have fallen! Repent and do the things you did at first." **Revelation 2:4-5***

DEVOTIONAL

It's never too late to reconnect with your first love—whether it's a passion, a dream, or a relationship—by nurturing it just like you would a cherished garden.

DAILY REFLECTION

What activities or moments brought you pure joy and felt closest to God when you first fell in love with Him? How can you incorporate those experiences into your life today?

PRAYER

Dear Lord, thank you for your unwavering love and the joy of our first connection. Help me to rekindle that passion in my heart and draw me closer to you each day.

Returning to my first love means rediscovering the joy of intimacy with God, just as I would nurture the fond memories of my youth.

July 24

Perseverance Through Prayer

"Be joyful in hope, patient in affliction, faithful in prayer."
Romans 12:12

DEVOTIONAL

Perseverance through prayer allows you to find strength and direction amidst life's storms.

DAILY REFLECTION

What do you feel God might be asking you to persist in prayer about today, even when the answers seem delayed? How can you trust His timing and plan in the waiting?

PRAYER

Dear Lord, thank You for always hearing my prayers. Help me to stay steadfast in my conversations with You, knowing that every word matters, and every moment of waiting shapes my heart.

Perseverance through prayer is not about the length of time spent in prayer, but the depth of trust we cultivate in those moments.

July 25

Flourishing in Every Season

"Consider the lilies of the field, how they grow; they toil not, neither do they spin. And yet I say unto you, that even Solomon in all his glory was not arrayed like one of these." **Matthew 6:28-29**

DEVOTIONAL

Embrace the unique gifts of each stage in your life, knowing that you are designed to thrive no matter the circumstances."

DAILY REFLECTION

What are the areas in your life where you feel you are struggling to flourish, and how can you invite God to nurture growth there?

PRAYER

Dear God, thank You for being the gardener of our hearts. Help us to trust in Your timing and to embrace every season of our lives with grace and joy.

Even in the shadows, there is potential for vibrant growth.

July 26

God's Presence in Your Routine

"Where can I go from your Spirit? Where can I flee from your presence? If I go up to the heavens, you are there; if I make my bed in the depths, you are there. If I rise on the wings of the dawn, if I settle on the far side of the sea, even there your hand will guide me, your right hand will hold me fast."
Psalm 139:7-10

DEVOTIONAL

Even in the routine, God's presence is a quiet reassurance that infuses love and purpose into each moment.

DAILY REFLECTION

What does it look like for you to invite God into the ordinary tasks of your daily routine? Can you identify moments when His presence feels especially close?

PRAYER

Dear Lord, thank you for walking with me through the daily rhythms of life. Help me to recognize and cherish Your presence in each moment, even amidst the mundane.

In the midst of the routine, His whispers invite us to be fully present.

July 27

Living with Holy Confidence

*"So do not throw away your confidence; it will be richly rewarded. You need to persevere so that when you have done the will of God, you will receive what He has promised." **Hebrews 10:35-36***

DEVOTIONAL

Living with holy confidence means recognizing that your strength is not derived from your circumstances, but from your relationship with God and His promises for your life.

DAILY REFLECTION

What does it mean for you to walk confidently in your daily life, embracing your role as a mom and a woman of faith? How does this confidence shape your interactions with others and your perspective on challenges?

PRAYER

Dear God, help me to embrace the holy confidence that comes from knowing I am loved and valued by You. Guide my heart and mind as I navigate the joys and challenges of motherhood, and remind me of the strength that lies within Your presence.

Confidence is not perfection: it's the quiet assurance that I am enough. just as I am.

July 28

Releasing the Weights You Carry

"Cast your cares on the Lord and He will sustain you."
Psalm 55:22

DEVOTIONAL

Life is too precious to bear the weight of expectations; by releasing those burdens, you create space for joy and connection in your daily journey.

DAILY REFLECTION

What burdens have you been carrying that might be holding you back from fully embracing the joy and peace God has for you?

PRAYER

Heavenly Father, help me to lay down the weights I carry. Teach me to trust in Your strength and guidance as I seek to find freedom in Your love.

Sometimes, the greatest act of faith is to release what we cannot control.

July 29

Faith That Transforms

"Forget the former things; do not dwell on the past. See, I am doing a new thing! Now it springs up; do you not perceive it? I am making a way in the wilderness and streams in the wasteland." **Isaiah 43:18-19**

DEVOTIONAL

God calls us to step into a renewed future, reminding us that transformation often begins when we dare to let go of the past and cling to the hope of what's to come.

DAILY REFLECTION

What areas of your life are you longing to see transformed by faith, and how can you invite God into those spaces today?

PRAYER

Dear Lord, thank You for the promise of transformation in our lives. Help me to hold on to faith in the midst of challenges and to trust that You are at work in every moment.

Faith is not a destination, but a journey that unfolds as we trust in God's perfect plan.

July 30

Praise Before the Breakthrough

"Enter his gates with thanksgiving and his courts with praise; give thanks to him and praise his name." **Psalm 100:4**

DEVOTIONAL

When we choose to praise God before we see the resolution of our problems, we open ourselves to His presence, allowing hope and peace to fill the gaps in our lives.

DAILY REFLECTION

What burdens are you carrying today that you can offer up in praise, trusting God's timing for your breakthrough?

PRAYER

Dear Heavenly Father, thank You for being with us in every season of life. Help us to lift our voices in praise, even when the path seems unclear. May our hearts find joy in the promise of Your presence.

Praise is a pathway to our breakthrough, revealing faith in the midst of uncertainty.

July 31

Rooted in God's Truth

P"But whose delight is in the law of the Lord, and who meditates on His law day and night. That person is like a tree planted by streams of water, which yields its fruit in season and whose leaf does not wither—whatever they do prospers." **Psalm 1:2-3**

DEVOTIONAL

Being rooted in God's truth provides stability and nourishment amidst the chaos of daily life, reminding you that you are never alone in your journey.

DAILY REFLECTION

What does it mean for you to be truly rooted in God's truth amidst the busyness of motherhood and daily life? How can you bring that truth into your relationships and decisions today?

PRAYER

Dear God, thank You for the foundation of Your truth in my life. Help me to stay grounded in Your Word and to reflect Your love and wisdom to those around me.

Rooted in God's truth, we can weather any storm and nourish the seeds of love and hope in our families.

August 1

Confidence in His Plan

"Commit your way to the Lord; trust in him and he will do this."
Psalm 37:5

DEVOTIONAL

Trusting in His plan gives us the strength to navigate life's uncertainties with grace and confidence.

DAILY REFLECTION

What areas of your life are you struggling to trust God's plan for right now, and how can you invite Him into those moments?

PRAYER

Dear Lord, thank You for the unique and beautiful journey You have laid out for each of us. Help me to trust in Your plan and embrace each moment, knowing that You are always with me.

Sometimes, the greatest act of faith is simply to believe that God has a purpose, even when we can't see it.

August 2

When You Feel Spiritually Dry

"Though the mountains be shaken and the hills be removed, yet my unfailing love for you will not be shaken, nor my covenant of peace be removed," **Isaiah 54:1**

DEVOTIONAL

God's love is steadfast and unwavering, inviting us to return to Him even when our spirits feel parched.

DAILY REFLECTION

What moments in your life have felt spiritually barren, and how have you sought to connect with God during those times?

PRAYER

Dear God, in moments of dryness, help me to feel your presence surrounding me. Remind me that even in stillness, you are working in my heart and soul.

Even the desert has its hidden springs.

August 3

God Is in the Details

*1"For I know the plans I have for you, declares the Lord, plans to prosper you and not to harm you, plans to give you hope and a future." **Jeremiah 29:11***

DEVOTIONAL

Even in the busiest and messiest moments of life, God is working behind the scenes, inviting us to find Him in the details.

DAILY REFLECTION

What small details in your life today might be God's gentle reminders of His presence and care for you? How can you take a moment to appreciate them?

PRAYER

Dear Lord, thank You for the intricate details of our lives that remind us of Your love and faithfulness. Open our eyes to see You in every moment, and grant us the peace to embrace your plan.

In the quiet moments, God weaves His presence into the tapestry of our daily lives.

August 4

Letting Go of the Past

"...weeping may endure for a night, but joy comes in the morning."
Psalm 30:5

DEVOTIONAL

Letting go of the past opens the door to new beginnings and the joy that God has waiting for us.

DAILY REFLECTION

What burdens from your past are you still carrying, and how might releasing them free you to embrace the present? Consider how these memories shape your heart and spirit today. Are you ready to let them go?

PRAYER

Dear God, grant me the courage to release the weight of my past and embrace the beauty of today. Help me to trust in Your plan and to find peace in each step I take forward. Amen.

Letting go of the past is not forgetting; it's choosing to release its hold on your heart.

August 5

Choosing Faith in Uncertainty

"For nothing will be impossible with God."
Luke 1:37

DEVOTIONAL

When uncertainty looms, allowing faith to guide you can illuminate paths you never knew existed, revealing hope in even the darkest moments.

DAILY REFLECTION

What uncertainties are you facing in your life right now, and how might choosing faith transform your perspective on those challenges?

PRAYER

Dear God, thank you for being our anchor in the storm. Help me to trust you in the midst of uncertainty and to find peace in your promises each day.

Faith is the bridge we build when the path ahead is unclear.

August 6

You Are Seen and Known

"See what great love the Father has lavished on us, that we should be called children of God! And that is what we are!" **1 John 3:1**

DEVOTIONAL

You are cherished beyond measure, and your unique journey is recognized and valued, even in the mundane moments of life.

DAILY REFLECTION

What moments in your life have made you feel most deeply seen and understood? How can you invite those feelings into your everyday routines as a reminder of your worth and presence?

PRAYER

Dear Lord, remind us today that we are each known and cherished by You. Help us to embrace our identities as loved mothers and women, finding comfort in Your unending grace.

You are seen, you are known, and you are held
in the embrace of a love that knows no bounds.

August 7

The Strength of Quiet Obedience

"And whether you turn to the right or to the left, your ears will hear a voice behind you, saying, 'This is the way; walk in it." **Isaiah 30:21**

DEVOTIONAL

In the stillness of obedience, we often discover the loudest echoes of God's guidance.

DAILY REFLECTION

What does quiet obedience look like in your life, and how can it lead you to greater peace and strength during your daily challenges?

PRAYER

Dear God, thank you for guiding me in moments where silence speaks louder than words. Help me embrace the power of quiet obedience in my heart and actions each day.

Within the stillness of the soul,
God whispers the strength we need to follow Him.

August 8

Refined by Fire

"These trials will show that your faith is genuine. It is being tested as fire tests and purifies gold—though your faith is far more precious than mere gold." **1 Peter 1:7**

DEVOTIONAL

Just as gold is refined in fire, the challenges you face are shaping you into the beautiful, strong woman you are becoming.

DAILY REFLECTION

What challenges have you faced recently that might feel like a refining fire, and how can you lean into those moments to grow stronger and more resilient?

PRAYER

Dear God, thank you for the journey you have placed before me. Help me to embrace the heat of life's challenges, trusting that you are shaping me into the woman you desire me to be.

Through the flames, I am being forged into my truest self.

August 9

God's Grace in Your Weakness

"For by grace you have been saved through faith, and that not of yourselves; it is the gift of God, not of works, lest anyone should boast."
Ephesians 2:8-9

DEVOTIONAL

We are never alone in our weaknesses; instead, it is in those very moments that God's grace shines the brightest, reminding us that it is okay not to be okay.

DAILY REFLECTION

What areas of your life make you feel vulnerable or insufficient, and how might you invite God's grace into those spaces?

PRAYER

Dear God, thank you for your grace that meets us in our weaknesses. Help us to embrace our flaws and trust in your strength to carry us through.

In our weakest moments, God's grace shines the brightest.

August 10

Living Intentionally

"Let your reasonableness be known to everyone. The Lord is at hand; do not be anxious about anything, but in everything by prayer and supplication with thanksgiving let your requests be made known to God."
Philippians 4:5-6

DEVOTIONAL

Embrace the beauty of each day by living intentionally, prioritizing moments that nourish your soul and relationships.

DAILY REFLECTION

What small, intentional choice can you make today to prioritize your well-being and the well-being of your family?

PRAYER

Dear Lord, help me to embrace each moment with intention. Guide my heart and mind to focus on the relationships and activities that truly matter, and grant me the strength to make choices that align with Your purpose for my life.

Intentional living is the daily choice to fill our moments with purpose and love.

August 11

The Joy of the Lord Is Your Strength

"The joy of the Lord is your strength."
Nehemiah 8:10

DEVOTIONAL

Seek joy, not just for yourself but as a reservoir of strength to uplift your family.

DAILY REFLECTION

What brings you joy in your daily life, and how can you lean into those moments to draw strength from them?

PRAYER

Dear Lord, thank you for the joy You bring into our lives, even in the ordinary moments. Help us to embrace that joy as a source of strength and encouragement throughout our day.

*True strength flows from the joy we accept
as a gift from God, even in our everyday challenges.*

August 12

Clinging to What Is Good

"Hold on to what is good, reject every kind of evil."
1 Thessalonians 5:21-22

DEVOTIONAL

In the busyness of life, it's essential to intentionally seek out and hold onto the moments and people that bring you love, joy, and peace.

DAILY REFLECTION

What are the good things in your life that you can cherish and hold onto, even amidst the chaos of motherhood and daily responsibilities?

PRAYER

Dear Heavenly Father, help me to recognize and appreciate the goodness in my life. As I navigate through the busyness, may I find comfort and strength in the blessings around me. Amen.

Clinging to what is good helps anchor our hearts in the storm.

August 13

Faithful in the Small Things

"Whoever can be trusted with very little can also be trusted with much."
Luke 16:10

DEVOTIONAL

The small, seemingly insignificant actions of our daily lives carry the potential to create profound change in ourselves and others.

DAILY REFLECTION

What small task or responsibility in your daily life feels insignificant, yet you know it matters to God and your family? How can you approach it with renewed faithfulness today?

PRAYER

Dear Lord, thank You for the little moments that shape our days and our hearts. Help me to see the value in the small things and to remain faithful, knowing that in doing so, I am serving You and my family.

Great faithfulness is often found in the simple acts of love we offer each day.

August 14

Harvesting Spiritual Growth

"The harvest is plentiful, but the workers are few. Ask the Lord of the harvest, therefore, to send out workers into his harvest field."
Matthew 9:37-38

DEVOTIONAL

Nourish your spiritual well-being daily, for just as a garden needs tending, so does your heart and spirit.

DAILY REFLECTION

What areas of your spiritual life feel like they are ready for harvest? What steps can you take to nurture that growth?

PRAYER

Dear Lord, thank You for the seeds of faith You have sown in my heart. Help me to tend to my spiritual garden, nourishing my growth with Your love and light.

Every season of nurturing leads to a bountiful harvest.

August 15

The Beauty of Surrender

"Trust in the Lord with all your heart and lean not on your own understanding; in all your ways submit to him, and he will make your paths straight." **Proverbs 3:5-6**

DEVOTIONAL

Surrendering to God doesn't signify weakness; it opens the door to deeper peace and trust in the beautiful chaos of motherhood.

DAILY REFLECTION

What does it look like for you to surrender your daily worries and embrace the peace that comes with trust in God's plan for your life? How can you invite Him into the moments where you feel most overwhelmed?

PRAYER

Heavenly Father, thank You for the invitation to surrender and trust in Your perfect will. Help me to rest in Your love and to let go of my worries, knowing that You hold my future in Your capable hands.

Surrendering is not a loss of control,
but a beautiful exchange of our burdens for His peace.

August 16

He Works All Things for Good

"...in all things God works for the good of those who love him, who have been called according to his purpose." **Romans 8:28**

DEVOTIONAL

The comforting truth is that even when life feels chaotic and plans unravel, God uses every experience to shape us—and those we love—into something beautiful.

DAILY REFLECTION

What are the difficult situations in your life that you can surrender to God, trusting that He is weaving them into your story for a greater purpose? How can you remind yourself of His faithfulness in these moments?

PRAYER

Dear Lord, thank You for Your promise that You work all things for good. Help me to trust in Your plan, even when I can't see it, and to find peace in knowing that You hold my life in Your hands.

Every thread of our lives is woven with purpose,
creating a beautiful tapestry only God can see.

August 17

A Steadfast Spirit

"Surely the righteous will never be shaken; they will be remembered forever. They will have no fear of bad news; their hearts are steadfast, trusting in the Lord." **Psalm 112:5-7**

DEVOTIONAL

When we cultivate a steadfast spirit, we can face life's uncertainties with grace and resilience, knowing that our trust in God steadies us through every storm.

DAILY REFLECTION

What does it mean for you to have a steadfast spirit in the face of life's challenges, and how can you cultivate that strength in your daily routine?

PRAYER

Dear Lord, thank You for the strength You provide. Help me to cultivate a steadfast spirit, grounded in Your love and grace, as I navigate the responsibilities and joys of motherhood and life.

A steadfast spirit is a heart anchored in faith, unshaken by the winds of change.

August 18

Hope That Holds

"We have this hope as an anchor for the soul, firm and secure."
Hebrews 6:19

DEVOTIONAL

True hope is not found in the absence of challenges but in the knowledge that we are held and guided through them.

DAILY REFLECTION

What are the hopes you hold onto in your life right now, and how can trusting in God's promises help strengthen those hopes?

PRAYER

Dear Lord, thank You for the hope that anchors our souls. Help us to remember that our dreams and desires, when filtered through Your will, can bring peace and purpose.

Hope is the quiet confidence that tomorrow holds possibilities beyond our imagination.

August 19

Casting Your Cares

"And surely I am with you always, to the very end of the age."
Matthew 28:20

DEVOTIONAL

Even in the busiest seasons of life, remember that His presence brings solace; you are never alone in your journey.

DAILY REFLECTION

What moments in your life remind you that you are never alone, even amid challenges and joy?

PRAYER

Dear Lord, thank you for your constant presence in my life. Help me to recognize your love in every moment, guiding me with peace and assurance.

His presence is the gentle whisper in the chaos of motherhood.

August 20

He Is with You Always

"And surely I am with you always, to the very end of the age."
Matthew 28:20

DEVOTIONAL

In every tumultuous moment of motherhood, remember that His unwavering presence is your anchor, reminding you that you are never alone.

DAILY REFLECTION

What does it mean for you to feel God's presence in your daily life, especially during moments of joy or challenge? How can you invite Him into the ordinary moments of your day?

PRAYER

Dear God, thank You for being with me always, in every moment of my life. Help me to recognize Your presence more vividly today and to find comfort and strength in knowing that I am never alone.

His presence is the anchor in your storm and the light in your path.

August 21

Walking in His Truth

"Let love and faithfulness never leave you; bind them around your neck, write them on the tablet of your heart. Then you will win favor and a good name in the sight of God and man." **Proverbs 3:3-4**

DEVOTIONAL

Walking in His truth allows us to prioritize love and faithfulness, creating a life of peace amid chaos.

DAILY REFLECTION

What does it mean for you to walk in His truth in your daily life, amidst the challenges and joys of motherhood?

PRAYER

Dear Lord, as I navigate the path of motherhood, help me to embrace Your truth in every moment. Fill my heart with peace and clarity as I seek to honor You through my actions and words.

Walking in His truth transforms our daily steps into a sacred journey filled with grace and purpose.

August 22

Forgiveness Is Freedom

"Be kind to one another, tenderhearted, forgiving one another, as God in Christ forgave you." **Ephesians 4:32**

DEVOTIONAL

Forgiveness is a powerful choice that, when embraced, opens the door to true freedom and an authentic life filled with love and joy.

DAILY REFLECTION

What burdens are you holding onto that keep you from experiencing true freedom?

PRAYER

Dear God, thank you for the gift of forgiveness. Help me to release the weight of past grievances and embrace the lightness that comes with letting go.

Forgiveness is not just a gift to others; it's a pathway to your own freedom.

August 23

Bearing Spiritual Fruit

"That person is like a tree planted by streams of water, which yields its fruit in season and whose leaf does not wither—whatever they do prospers."
Psalm 1:3

DEVOTIONAL

The fruits of our labor often appear in the lessons we teach, the love we share, and the lives we touch, even when we cannot see them immediately.

DAILY REFLECTION

What areas of your life are ripe for growth, and how can you nurture them to bear spiritual fruit?

PRAYER

Dear Lord, thank you for the gift of this day and the opportunities it brings. Help me to cultivate the soil of my heart so that I can produce the fruits of the Spirit in my life and in those around me.

When we cultivate our hearts with love, joy, and kindness, we create a garden that blesses the world.

August 24

The Peace of Letting Go

"Therefore do not worry about tomorrow, for tomorrow will worry about itself. Each day has enough trouble of its own." **Matthew 6:34**

DEVOTIONAL

Sometimes, the greatest peace comes from the courage to release what we cannot control.

DAILY REFLECTION

What burdens are you carrying that you need to let go of in order to embrace the peace God offers you?

PRAYER

Lord, grant me the courage to release my worries and trust in Your plan. Help me to embrace the serenity that comes with surrendering my burdens to You, knowing that Your guidance is always with me.

True peace comes when we release the need to control and allow God to lead.

August 25

Strength to Begin Again

*"Though she may stumble, she will not fall,
for the Lord upholds her with His hand."* **Psalm 37:24**

DEVOTIONAL

Embrace the courage to start anew; every beginning is a chance to
rediscover the vibrant soul within you.

DAILY REFLECTION

*What new beginnings are you feeling called to embrace right now, and
how can you take the first step towards them today?*

PRAYER

Dear God, grant her the strength to let go of the past and courage to step
into new beginnings with a heart full of hope. May she feel Your loving
presence guiding her every step.

Every ending is a prelude to a new beginning: embrace the change.

August 26

Your Life Is a Testimony

*"Surely your goodness and mercy shall follow me all the days of my life,
and I shall dwell in the house of the LORD forever."* **Psalm 23:6**

DEVOTIONAL

Remember, your experiences are not just for you: they can offer hope and
encouragement to those around you who may be struggling or seeking
direction.

DAILY REFLECTION

*What story is your life telling to those around you? How can your
experiences inspire others to see the beauty of faith in everyday moments?*

PRAYER

Dear God, thank you for the unique journey you have paved in my life. Help
me to recognize and share the lessons that can uplift those around me,
shining your light through my testimony.

*Your life is a living testament to the grace
that has carried you through.*

August 27

Restoring Joy

"For everything there is a season, and a time for every matter under heaven: a time to weep, and a time to laugh; a time to mourn, and a time to dance." **Ecclesiastes 3:1–4**

DEVOTIONAL

Sometimes, amidst the chaos of motherhood and life's demands, we must create space for joy to resurface in our hearts.

DAILY REFLECTION

What brings you joy in your life right now, and how can you nurture that joy amidst the demands of motherhood and daily responsibilities? Reflect on the small moments that make you smile—are you allowing yourself to fully embrace them?

PRAYER

Lord, thank You for the simple joys that fill our days. Help me to recognize and cherish these moments, finding restoration in Your presence and peace in my heart.

Joy is not a destination; it's a daily choice to see the beauty around us.

August 28

God's Power in Your Story

"He gives strength to the weary and increases the power of the weak. Even youths grow tired and weary, and young men stumble and fall; but those who hope in the Lord will renew their strength. They will soar on wings like eagles; they will run and not grow weary, they will walk and not be faint."
Isaiah 40:29–31

DEVOTIONAL

Your life is a tapestry of experiences, both beautiful and challenging, and God's power is intricately woven within each thread.

DAILY REFLECTION

What unique moments in your life have shaped you, revealing God's power in your story? Can you see how your experiences have prepared you for the present season?

PRAYER

Dear God, thank You for being the author of our stories. Help us recognize Your power at work in our lives, and grant us the courage to share our journey with others.

Your story is a testament of grace, where God's power transforms every chapter into a masterpiece.

August 29

Enduring with Grace

"For I consider that the sufferings of this present time are not worth comparing with the glory that is to be revealed to us." **Romans 8:18**

DEVOTIONAL

Even amidst the everyday chaos of life, your strength and grace shine brighter than you realize, nurturing those around you and cultivating hope for tomorrow.

DAILY REFLECTION

What does enduring with grace look like in your everyday life, and how can you invite God into those moments of challenge?

PRAYER

Dear Lord, help her to embrace each day with strength and grace. Surround her with Your love and wisdom as she navigates life's ups and downs. Let her feel Your presence in her heart and give her the courage to endure.

Grace is the quiet strength that carries us through life's storms.

August 30

Preparing for a New Season

"Therefore, if anyone is in Christ, the new creation has come: The old has gone, the new is here!" **2 Corinthians 5:17**

DEVOTIONAL

Embrace the new season of your life with hope, knowing that it holds opportunities for growth and joy.

DAILY REFLECTION

What are the areas of your life that feel ready for change, and how can you embrace this new season with grace and courage?

PRAYER

Dear God, thank you for the new seasons in our lives and the growth they bring. Help us to embrace change, filling our hearts with hope and our minds with peace as we step into what You have in store for us.

Every season carries a unique purpose:
trust in the unfolding of your journey.

August 31

Entering a New Season with Faith

"But those who hope in the Lord will renew their strength. They will soar on wings like eagles; they will run and not grow weary, they will walk and not be faint." **Isaiah 40:31**

DEVOTIONAL

Embrace the new season of your life with courage, knowing that your faith can guide you to new beginnings and deeper fulfillment.

DAILY REFLECTION

What new opportunities or challenges is God inviting you to embrace in this next season of your life? How can you lean into your faith during this transition?

PRAYER

Dear Lord, as I step into this new season, help me to embrace the changes with open arms and trust in Your guidance. Fill my heart with peace and strength as I journey forward, knowing that You are with me every step of the way.

Faith is the bridge that takes us from where we are to where God wants us to be.

September 1

Resting in God's Rhythm

"Come to me, all you who are weary and burdened, and I will give you rest. Take my yoke upon you and learn from me, for I am gentle and humble in heart, and you will find rest for your souls. For my yoke is easy and my burden is light." **Matthew 11:28–30**

DEVOTIONAL

In the whirlwind of life, remember that resting in God's rhythm means allowing Him to shoulder your burdens while you nurture your spirit.

DAILY REFLECTION

What does it look like for you to truly rest in God's rhythm during your busy days as a mom?

PRAYER

Lord, help me to quiet my heart and mind, recognizing the beauty of resting in Your presence. Teach me to embrace Your rhythm and find peace in each moment.

Resting in God's rhythm allows us to find joy in each day's unfolding.

September 2

When You Feel Behind

"Martha, Martha, you are worried and upset about many things, but few things are needed—or indeed only one. Mary has chosen what is better, and it will not be taken away from her." **Luke 10:41–42**

DEVOTIONAL

It's okay to pause and realign your focus; true peace and fulfillment come not from relentless busyness but from intentional living.

DAILY REFLECTION

What areas of your life do you feel are lagging behind expectations or desires? How can you reframe those feelings to find peace in your journey?

PRAYER

Dear Lord, help me to embrace the rhythm of my life without comparison. Grant me the strength to trust in Your perfect timing and purpose for my story.

Your journey is uniquely yours, and each step, no matter how small, contributes to the masterpiece God is creating.

September 3

Seeking God First

*"But seek first his kingdom and his righteousness, and all these things will be given to you as well." **Matthew 6:33***

DEVOTIONAL

In the midst of motherhood and life's demands, prioritizing time with God can transform your perspective and provide the strength you need to navigate your journey.

DAILY REFLECTION

What does seeking God first look like in your everyday life, especially as a busy mom? How can you carve out moments in your routine to prioritize your spiritual connection and trust in Him?

PRAYER

Dear Lord, help me to prioritize my relationship with You amidst the demands of motherhood and daily life. May I find joy in seeking You first and rest in Your presence.

By putting God at the forefront of our lives, we discover a peace and clarity that shapes all our decisions.

September 4

You Are Never Alone

"The Lord himself goes before you and will be with you; he will never leave you nor forsake you. Do not be afraid; do not be discouraged."
Deuteronomy 31:8

DEVOTIONAL

Remember, dear friend, even in your busiest or loneliest moments, you are never truly alone; God is always there, cheering you on and loving you deeply.

DAILY REFLECTION

What moment in your day feels the loneliest, and how can you invite God into that space to remind you of His presence?

PRAYER

Dear God, thank you for always being with us, especially in moments of solitude. Help us to feel your love and guidance as we navigate the complexities of motherhood and life. Amen.

In every heartbeat, remember: You are cradled in love, surrounded by the unseen hand that holds your heart.

September 5

Refreshed by His Presence

"You make known to me the path of life; in your presence there is fullness of joy; at your right hand are pleasures forevermore." **Psalm 16:11**

DEVOTIONAL

Look for those moments of stillness amidst the busyness; they are not just breaks but invitations to experience His refreshing presence.

DAILY REFLECTION

What moments in your day can you intentionally set aside to encounter God's presence and be refreshed by His love?

PRAYER

Dear Lord, thank you for your constant presence in our lives. Help us to seek you amid the busyness, finding peace and joy in the time we spend with you.

In the quiet moments, His presence
is a gentle reminder of who we truly are.

September 6

Trusting God's Bigger Picture

"And my God will meet all your needs according to the riches of his glory in Christ Jesus." **Philippians 4:19**

DEVOTIONAL

You may not see the bigger picture today, but trust that God is crafting something magnificent beyond your understanding.

DAILY REFLECTION

What are some areas in your life where you're struggling to trust in God's bigger picture, and how can you take a step towards surrendering that burden to Him?

PRAYER

Dear Lord, help me to see beyond my immediate worries and to trust in Your perfect plan. Give me the strength to lean into Your guidance and the peace that comes from knowing You're always working for my good.

Faith is not believing that God will do what you ask,
but trusting that He will do what is best.

September 7

The Fruit of the Spirit

*"But the fruit of the Spirit is love, joy, peace, forbearance, kindness, goodness, faithfulness, gentleness, and self-control." **Galatians 5:22-23***

DEVOTIONAL

As you journey through the demands of life, remember that each moment is an opportunity to cultivate the fruit of the Spirit within you, turning everyday challenges into beautiful lessons of love and grace.

DAILY REFLECTION

What does it mean for you to cultivate the Fruit of the Spirit in your daily life, and how can you intentionally nurture these qualities as a mother and friend?

PRAYER

Dear God, help me to embody the fruits of your Spirit in every area of my life. May your love, joy, and peace shine through me as I navigate motherhood and relationships. Thank you for the grace to grow and bear good fruit each day.

*True strength lies in the gentleness of the Spirit;
let love be your guiding force.*

September 8

A Faith That Grows

"But blessed is the one who trusts in the Lord, whose confidence is in him. They will be like a tree planted by the water that sends out its roots by the stream. It does not fear when heat comes; its leaves are always green. It has no worries in a year of drought and never fails to bear fruit."
Jeremiah 17:7-8

DEVOTIONAL

Faith isn't just about believing in God; it's a dynamic journey of growth and resilience through every season of life.

DAILY REFLECTION

What are some ways you've seen your faith grow over the years, and how can you nurture that growth even more in your current season of life?

PRAYER

Dear God, thank You for the journey of faith that unfolds in our lives. Help me to recognize and embrace the ways You are encouraging my heart to grow deeper in trust and love. Amen.

*Faith is not a destination, but a journey
that flourishes with every step we take.*

September 9

Finding Joy in Serving

"And if you spend yourselves in behalf of the hungry and satisfy the needs of the oppressed, then your light will rise in the darkness, and your night will become like the noonday." Isaiah 58:10

DEVOTIONAL

Finding joy in serving others often transforms our weariness into a renewed sense of purpose.

DAILY REFLECTION

What activities in your life bring you joy when you serve others, and how can you incorporate more of those moments into your daily routine? Reflect on the ways your unique gifts can shine in service to your family and community.

PRAYER

Dear God, thank You for the opportunity to serve those around me. Help me to find joy in each act of kindness and to recognize the beauty in the simple moments spent giving to others.

Joy blooms where love is freely given.

September 10

God Is Your Shelter

"Whoever dwells in the secret place of the Most High will rest in the shadow of the Almighty. I will say of the Lord, 'He is my refuge and my fortress, my God, in whom I trust.'" Psalm 91:1-2

DEVOTIONAL

Remember, no matter how busy or chaotic life may become, turning to God as your shelter will bring you the peace and strength you need to weather any storm.

DAILY REFLECTION

What does it mean to you to find shelter in God during the storms of your life? Can you recall a specific moment when you felt His protection and comfort surrounding you?

PRAYER

Dear Lord, thank You for being my refuge and my strength. Help me to remember that no matter what challenges come my way, I can always find my safe place in You.

In the embrace of God's love, you are forever sheltered.

September 11

The Power of Your Words

"The tongue has the power of life and death, and those who love it will eat its fruit." **Proverbs 18:21**

DEVOTIONAL

Our words have the extraordinary ability to either build up or tear down, so choose to speak life, especially into those you love the most.

DAILY REFLECTION

What words have you spoken recently that uplifted someone? How can you make a conscious effort today to speak life into those around you?

PRAYER

Lord, help me to recognize the power of my words. May I use them to bring comfort, encouragement, and love to those I encounter today.

Your words have the power to create an atmosphere of hope and joy.

September 12

Returning to God's Heart

"I will give them a heart to know me, that I am the Lord; and they shall be my people, and I will be their God, for they shall return to me with their whole heart." **Jeremiah 24:7**

DEVOTIONAL

In the busyness of life, remember that your heart will always long for the safety and love found in returning to God.

DAILY REFLECTION

What is one way you can peel back the layers of your busy life to reconnect with God's heart today?

PRAYER

Dear God, as I seek Your presence, help me to quiet the noise around me and listen for Your whisper. Bring me closer to Your heart and fill me with Your love and guidance.

To return to God's heart is to find the home where your soul is truly nourished.

September 13

Every Season Has Purpose

Isaiah 61:3 offers us a beautiful reminder that God brings beauty from ashes and joy from mourning, revealing His profound purpose in every season we encounter.

DEVOTIONAL

Embrace each moment, for every season carries within it the seeds of purpose that will bloom in ways you may not yet understand.

DAILY REFLECTION

What season of life are you currently navigating, and how can you embrace the purpose within this moment?

PRAYER

Dear God, thank you for the seasons you bring into our lives. Help me to see the beauty and purpose in each one, knowing that you are with me through it all.

Embrace the unfolding of your life, for each moment has the power to shape the woman you are meant to be.

September 14

Living with Spiritual Clarity

"The beginning of wisdom is this: Get wisdom. Though it cost all you have, get understanding." **Proverbs 4:7**

DEVOTIONAL

When you feel overwhelmed, remember that clarity comes from intentional moments of stillness; prioritize your inner life, for it shapes your outer journey.

DAILY REFLECTION

What does spiritual clarity look like in your daily life, and how can you cultivate that clarity amidst the busyness of motherhood and other responsibilities?

PRAYER

Dear God, guide me to see Your presence in the chaos of my day. Help me to find peace in the choices I make and to trust in Your wisdom as I navigate my path.

Clarity comes not from the absence of chaos, but from the presence of faith.

September 15

Letting God Carry the Load

"Rejoice in the Lord and let your gentleness be evident to all. The Lord is near. Do not be anxious about anything, but in every situation, by prayer and petition, with thanksgiving, present your requests to God."
Philippians 4:4-6

DEVOTIONAL

Letting God carry the load means allowing yourself the freedom to lean on His strength when life feels too heavy.

DAILY REFLECTION

What burdens are you carrying today that you could hand over to God? How might your life change if you let Him take the weight of those worries?

PRAYER

Dear God, please help me to trust You with my burdens. Teach me to release my worries into Your capable hands, knowing that You care for me deeply. May I feel Your peace enveloping me as I let go.

Sometimes the strongest thing we can do is to simply let go and let God.

September 16

Hope in the Hidden Places

"The Lord will guide you continually, giving you water when you are dry and restoring your strength. You will be like a well-watered garden, like an ever-flowing spring." **Isaiah 58:11**

DEVOTIONAL

Hope often thrives in the mundane; look for it in the hidden places of your heart and soul, for it has the power to rejuvenate your spirit.

DAILY REFLECTION

What hidden places in your life could use a little more hope today? How can you invite God into those spaces to bring light and renewal?

PRAYER

Dear Lord, we thank You for being the light in our hidden places. Fill our hearts with hope and help us to trust in Your perfect timing and unfailing love.

Even in the shadows, God's light can create beauty where we least expect it.

September 17

Obedient in the Unknown

"...faith is confidence in what we hope for and assurance about what we do not see." **Hebrews 11:1**

DEVOTIONAL

In the unknown spaces of our lives, obedience often opens doors to blessings we never expected.

DAILY REFLECTION

What unknown paths are you currently walking in your life, and how can trusting in God's wisdom guide you through these uncertainties?

PRAYER

Dear Lord, as I navigate through the unknown, help me to seek Your guidance and embrace the journey ahead. Teach me to trust in Your plan, even when the path is unclear.

Faith in the face of uncertainty opens the door to new possibilities.

September 18

He Redeems Every Chapter

"But I will restore you to health and heal your wounds,"
Jeremiah 30:17:

DEVOTIONAL

Every chapter of your life holds significance; trust that God is weaving your story with grace and purpose.

DAILY REFLECTION

What chapters of your life feel unresolved or unworthy of redemption? How might you invite God into these spaces to create a new narrative?

PRAYER

Dear Lord, thank You for the promise that You redeem every chapter of our lives. Help me to trust in Your perfect plan and to see the beauty in the places where I feel broken. I open my heart to Your healing and guidance today.

Every page turned is a testament to grace;
God's hand weaves stories of hope where we see only despair.

September 19

You Are Fully Known and Loved

"You have searched me, Lord, and you know me. You know when I sit and when I rise; you perceive my thoughts from afar. You discern my going out and my lying down; you are familiar with all my ways. Before a word is on my tongue, you, Lord, know it completely." **Psalm 139:1-4**

DEVOTIONAL

You are deeply known and loved, both in your beautiful complexity and in the simplicity of being just who you are.

DAILY REFLECTION

What does it mean for you to be fully known and loved by God? In what ways do you feel that truth manifest in your life as a mom and a woman today?

PRAYER

Dear God, thank you for knowing every part of my heart and life. Help me to embrace your love deeply and to extend that love to those around me.

In your most vulnerable moments,
remember that you are cherished beyond measure.

September 20

Praise as a Weapon

"Let everything that has breath praise the Lord! Praise the Lord."
Psalm 150:6

DEVOTIONAL

When you wield praise as a weapon, you cultivate an environment where peace, strength, and joy flourish amidst life's storms.

DAILY REFLECTION

What challenges are you currently facing that might seem overwhelming, and how can turning to praise shift your perspective and strengthen your spirit?

PRAYER

Dear God, help me to remember the strength I have in You. May my praises uplift my spirit and refocus my heart, even in the midst of life's storms. Thank You for being my constant source of hope.

Praise transforms our battles into victories, shifting our focus
from the giants we face to the greatness of our God.

September 21

Unshaken in the Storm

"As for God, His way is perfect; the word of the Lord is tried: He is a buckler to all them that trust in Him." **2 Samuel 22:31**

DEVOTIONAL

In the midst of life's storms, remember that your faith can be your strongest refuge.

DAILY REFLECTION

What storms are currently swirling in your life, and how can you find peace amidst the chaos? Consider ways you can lean into your faith for strength and stability.

PRAYER

Dear Lord, grant me the courage to stand firm in the face of life's storms. Help me to find comfort in Your presence and to trust that You are my anchor.

Even amid the fiercest storms, my spirit remains anchored in faith.

September 22

Choosing to Trust Again

"Taste and see that the Lord is good; blessed is the one who takes refuge in him." **Psalm 34:8**

DEVOTIONAL

Choosing to trust again means embracing hope over fear and recognizing the goodness that awaits beyond our past pains.

DAILY REFLECTION

What experiences in your life have made it difficult for you to trust again, and how can you take small steps towards rebuilding that trust today?

PRAYER

Dear Lord, help me to release my fears and open my heart to trust once more. Grant me the courage to embrace new beginnings with faith and hope.

Trust is not the absence of fear, but the choice to believe despite it.

September 23

Walking in Spiritual Wisdom

"For the Lord gives wisdom; from His mouth come knowledge and understanding." **Proverbs 2:6**

DEVOTIONAL

Seek God in every moment, for His wisdom will transform your chaos into a beautiful tapestry of grace.

DAILY REFLECTION

What does it mean for you to walk in spiritual wisdom in your daily life, and how can you invite God into your decisions today?

PRAYER

Dear God, thank You for the gift of Your wisdom that guides us each day. Help me to trust in Your direction and to discern Your truth in every choice I face.

Spiritual wisdom is not just knowledge:
it's the ability to see life through God's eyes.

September 24

The Blessing of Surrender

"Commit to the Lord whatever you do, and he will establish your plans."
Proverbs 16:3

DEVOTIONAL

Surrendering to God isn't a sign of weakness; it's an invitation to experience His strength in our lives.

DAILY REFLECTION

What does surrender look like in your life right now, and how could embracing it bring you peace and joy amidst the busyness of motherhood?

PRAYER

Dear God, help me to embrace the art of surrender in my everyday life. Grant me the wisdom to let go of control and trust in Your perfect plan for me and my family. May I find comfort in knowing that Your grace is sufficient for every need.

Surrender is the quiet strength that acknowledges
our limits and allows God's love to fill the gaps.

September 25

Your Life Is a Light

"That you may become blameless and harmless, children of God without fault in the midst of a crooked and perverse generation, among whom you shine as lights in the world, holding fast the word of life." **Philippians 2:15-16**

DEVOTIONAL

You have the power to light the way for others, and the very essence of your journey inspires those around you to embrace their own paths.

DAILY REFLECTION

What are some ways you can let your unique light shine in the lives of those around you, especially your family and friends?

PRAYER

Dear God, thank you for the light you've placed within me. Help me to share that light boldly and lovingly with those I encounter each day. Amen.

Your light is meant to illuminate the path for others,
revealing hope and encouragement along the way.

September 26

Comforted by God's Nearness

"The LORD is close to the brokenhearted and saves those who are crushed in spirit." **Psalm 34:18**

DEVOTIONAL

God's nearness is a constant source of strength, reminding us that even in our most challenging moments, we are never truly alone.

DAILY REFLECTION

What does it mean for you to feel God's presence in your everyday life, especially during moments of challenge or joy? Can you recall a time when you sensed His nearness?

PRAYER

Dear Lord, thank You for being ever-present in my life. Help me to recognize Your comfort and embrace Your love amidst the busyness of motherhood and daily responsibilities.

God's nearness transforms our trials into testimonies of grace.

September 27

Refined Through Waiting

"No discipline seems pleasant at the time, but painful. Later on, however, it produces a harvest of righteousness and peace for those who have been trained by it." **Hebrews 12:11**

DEVOTIONAL

While waiting can be challenging, it is often in those moments that we are being shaped and prepared for something beautiful and fulfilling.

DAILY REFLECTION

What areas of your life are you currently waiting on, and how might God be using this time to refine your heart and strengthen your faith?

PRAYER

Dear God, thank you for being with us in our waiting. Help us to trust your timing, recognizing the growth you desire to cultivate within us. Amen.

Waiting is not a waste;
it is a season of preparation for something beautiful.

September 28

Grace for the Process

"Blessed are those whose strength is in You, whose hearts are set on pilgrimage. As they pass through the Valley of Baka, they make it a place of springs; the autumn rains also cover it with pools. They go from strength to strength, till each appears before God in Zion." **Psalm 84:5-7**

DEVOTIONAL

Life is a journey, and with each twist and turn, remember to extend grace to yourself just as God does.

DAILY REFLECTION

What does it feel like to embrace the journey of growth in your life, acknowledging both the struggles and triumphs that shape who you are today?

PRAYER

Dear Lord, thank You for Your unwavering grace that walks with us through every season of life. Help us to find beauty in the process of becoming, trusting that You are always at work within us.

Grace isn't just what God gives us; it's also what He plants in us through the ups and downs of our daily lives.

September 29

Celebrating God's Faithfulness

"Let us hold unswervingly to the hope we profess, for He who promised is faithful." **Hebrews 10:23**

DEVOTIONAL

In times of uncertainty, remember to reflect on God's past faithfulness, as it will guide your heart and illuminate your path forward.

DAILY REFLECTION

What moments in your life have you witnessed God's faithfulness, even amidst challenges? How can you celebrate those moments today?

PRAYER

Dear God, thank you for your unwavering faithfulness in my life. Help me to open my eyes to the blessings around me and to celebrate your goodness in every circumstance.

God's faithfulness is a steadfast anchor in the storms of life. reminding us that we are never alone.

September 30

Finding Peace in the Unknown

"And after you have suffered a little while, the God of all grace, who has called you to his eternal glory in Christ, will himself restore, confirm, strengthen, and establish you." **1 Peter 5:10**

DEVOTIONAL

There is peace in surrendering our worries to God, trusting that He is guiding us through the uncertainties.

DAILY REFLECTION

What unknown situations in your life are causing you worry or anxiety right now? How might you invite peace into these moments by trusting in a greater plan?

PRAYER

Dear God, thank You for Your constant presence in our lives. Help us find peace as we navigate the uncertainties of our journeys, and remind us that You are always guiding us.

In the silence of uncertainty. peace finds its voice.

A Moment of Gratitude

If this devotional has brought moments of peace, strength, or reflection into your life, a short review on Amazon can help others discover it too.

devo.anchoredgraces.com/2026

Even a few words about your experience can make a meaningful difference.

Thank you for continuing this journey.

October 1

You Are Chosen

*"For He chose us in Him before the creation of the world to be holy and blameless in His sight. In love, He predestined us for adoption to sonship through Jesus Christ." **Ephesians 1:4-5***

DEVOTIONAL

Remember, dear friend, that you are chosen by a loving God who sees you beyond your roles – you are treasured for who you are, not just what you do.

DAILY REFLECTION

What does it mean to you to be chosen by God in your life as a woman and a mother? How does this truth impact the way you see your purpose and your daily routine?

PRAYER

Dear God, thank You for choosing me and for the unique path You've laid out before me. Help me to embrace my identity as Your beloved daughter and to walk in the light of that calling each day.

You are not just a passenger in this life:
you are the one chosen to steer your ship with grace and courage.

October 2

When You Need Direction

*"Show me your ways, Lord, teach me your paths. Guide me in your truth and teach me, for you are God my Savior, and my hope is in you all day long." **Psalm 25:4-5***

DEVOTIONAL

Sometimes, when faced with uncertainty, opening our hearts in honesty can help illuminate the direction God intends for us.

DAILY REFLECTION

What decisions are you facing right now that leave you feeling uncertain? How can you seek guidance in these moments so that you can step forward with confidence?

PRAYER

Dear Lord, I come before you with a heart seeking direction. Please illuminate the path ahead and grant me the wisdom to recognize your signs as I navigate these choices.

Direction often comes not from clarity,
but from trusting the process of unfolding.

October 3

Abiding Through the Chaos

"Abide in Me, and I in you. As the branch cannot bear fruit of itself, unless it abides in the vine, neither can you, unless you abide in Me." **John 15:4**

DEVOTIONAL

In the midst of life's chaos, abiding in God provides the strength and peace we need to navigate each day.

DAILY REFLECTION

What chaos in your life feels overwhelming right now, and how might you invite God's peace into that space?

PRAYER

Dear God, in the midst of our busy lives, help us to find rest in You. May Your peace fill our hearts and guide our steps as we navigate the chaos of everyday moments.

Abiding means finding stillness in the storm, resting in the assurance of God's presence.

October 4

The Strength to Say Yes

"He gives strength to the weary and increases the power of the weak."
Isaiah 40:29

DEVOTIONAL

Saying 'yes' can empower not just you but also inspire those you love to embrace growth and change.

DAILY REFLECTION

What is one opportunity you have been hesitant to embrace lately, and what would it mean for you to say yes to it? How might this decision impact your life and those around you?

PRAYER

Dear God, grant me the courage to step out in faith and say yes to the calling you have placed in my heart. Help me to trust in your wisdom and embrace the new opportunities ahead, even when they seem daunting.

Sometimes, the strength to say yes comes from recognizing the beauty that lies beyond our comfort zones.

October 5

God's Love Never Changes

"For I the Lord do not change; therefore you,
O children of Jacob, are not consumed." **Malachi 3:6**

DEVOTIONAL

God's unwavering love is the anchor we need to navigate life's uncertainties
and to remember that we are enough, just as we are.

DAILY REFLECTION

What moments in your life have you felt the unwavering presence of God's
love, even amidst change and uncertainty? How can you carry that
awareness into your daily routine as a reminder of His constant support?

PRAYER

Dear Lord, thank you for your unchanging love that surrounds me every day.
Help me to embrace that love and share it with my family and friends,
reminding them of your faithfulness.

God's love is the anchor that holds us steady in life's storms.

October 6

He Sees the Whole Picture

"I lift my eyes to the hills—where does my help come from? My help comes
from the Lord, the Maker of heaven and earth." **Psalm 121:1-2**

DEVOTIONAL

Trust that even when we feel lost in the details, He's weaving a tapestry of
grace that holds our entire journey in His capable hands.

DAILY REFLECTION

What areas of your life feel overwhelming right now, and how might
trusting in God's vision help you navigate them?

PRAYER

Dear Lord, thank You for being the ultimate Author of our lives. Help me to see
beyond today's trials and trust that You are orchestrating every detail for my
good.

God sees the whole picture,
even when our view is limited to just the frame.

October 7

A Heart Aligned with His

"For where your treasure is, there your heart will be also."
Matthew 6:21

DEVOTIONAL

Make a conscious effort today to invest your time and energy in what aligns your heart with His—cherishing moments and relationships that reflect His love.

DAILY REFLECTION

What does it mean for your heart to be in sync with His? How can you cultivate that alignment in your daily life while managing the demands of being a mom and caring for your family?

PRAYER

Dear Lord, help me to draw closer to You each day. May my heart be attuned to Your whispers, guiding me to reflect Your love and grace in my life and home. Thank You for Your faithfulness and presence.

Aligning your heart with His is not about perfection;
it's about devotion.

October 8

Living with Spiritual Courage

"Be strong and courageous. Do not be afraid; do not be discouraged, for the Lord your God will be with you wherever you go." **Joshua 1:9**

DEVOTIONAL

When you feel the weight of life pressing down, remember that God walks with you, giving you the strength to rise above your fears.

DAILY REFLECTION

What does spiritual courage look like in your daily life, and how can you choose to embrace it in the face of challenges or fears you encounter as a mother and individual?

PRAYER

Dear God, as I navigate my journey, please fill me with the courage to step forward with faith. Help me to trust in Your plan and to inspire those around me with love and resilience.

Courage is not the absence of fear,
but the decision to move forward despite it.

October 9

The Promise of Renewal

*"And I am certain that God, who began the good work within you, will continue his work until it is finally finished on the day when Christ Jesus returns." **Philippians 1:6***

DEVOTIONAL

Embrace this season as one of continual growth, where every challenge is an opportunity to bloom anew.

DAILY REFLECTION

What areas of your life are yearning for a fresh start, and how can you invite God into those spaces?

PRAYER

Dear Lord, thank you for the promise of renewal in our lives. Help me to embrace the changes ahead and trust in Your perfect plan. May Your grace guide me as I navigate this journey.

Every ending holds the seed of a new beginning.

October 10

Clothed in Dignity and Strength

"She sets about her work vigorously; her arms are strong for her tasks."
Proverbs 31:17

DEVOTIONAL

You may not always see it, but the diligent love and courage you pour into your daily life is the true essence of strength and beauty.

DAILY REFLECTION

What does being 'clothed in dignity and strength' look like in your everyday life, and how can you embrace this identity in your role as a mother and woman of faith?

PRAYER

Dear Lord, thank you for the beautiful strength and dignity you place within us. Help me to wear these qualities with confidence, reflecting your love and grace in all that I do.

True dignity comes from recognizing our worth in God's eyes, allowing strength to guide our actions.

October 11

Running the Race Well

"Let us not become weary in doing good, for at the proper time we will reap a harvest if we do not give up." **Galatians 6:9**

DEVOTIONAL

In the journey of motherhood and life, remember that perseverance in the little things leads to a flourishing spirit and a meaningful legacy.

DAILY REFLECTION

What does running the race well mean to you in this season of your life as a mom, and how can you embrace this journey with grace and purpose?

PRAYER

Dear Lord, thank you for the gift of this day and the strength you provide. Help me to run the race set before me with perseverance, embracing each moment as a precious opportunity to grow in love and faith.

Every step forward is a testament to your resilience and devotion.

October 12

Stillness in God's Presence

"Yes, my soul, find rest in God; my hope comes from him. Truly he is my rock and my salvation; he is my fortress, I will not be shaken." **Psalm 62:5-6**

DEVOTIONAL

Embracing moments of stillness can transform our chaotic lives into encounters with peace, reminding us that God is always with us, ready to offer His presence as our refuge.

DAILY REFLECTION

What does it feel like for you to truly stop and rest in God's presence amid the busyness of life?

PRAYER

Dear God, help me to find peace and stillness in my heart. Guide me to recognize Your presence throughout my day and to draw strength from that quiet connection.

In the stillness, I hear God's whispers of love and direction.

October 13

Your Faith Can Move Mountains

"For truly I tell you, if you have faith as small as a mustard seed, you can say to this mountain, 'Move from here to there,' and it will move. Nothing will be impossible for you." **Matthew 17:20**

DEVOTIONAL

Your faith, no matter how small, can light the way through life's challenges, empowering you to overcome obstacles and embrace the blessings ahead.

DAILY REFLECTION

What mountains in your life seem insurmountable right now? Take a moment to reflect on how your faith can help you navigate these challenges and lead you toward a path of hope and strength.

PRAYER

Dear Lord, thank You for the strength that comes from our faith. Help us to see the possibilities beyond our challenges and trust in Your guidance as we face each mountain.

Faith is the bridge that carries us over our mountains.

October 14

Let God Rewrite Your Story

"But the Lord said to Samuel, 'Do not consider his appearance or his height, for I have rejected him. The Lord does not look at the things people look at. People look at the outward appearance, but the Lord looks at the heart.'"
1 Samuel 16:7

DEVOTIONAL

The beauty of life is that with God, our stories can always be rewritten, no matter how old we are or what we've experienced.

DAILY REFLECTION

What parts of your story have you longed to rewrite, and how might inviting God into those areas bring you a renewed sense of hope and purpose?

PRAYER

Dear God, thank you for always being willing to rewrite our stories with love and grace. Help me to let go of my fears and embrace the new chapters you have in store for me.

Every new chapter in your life can bring healing, growth, and a beautiful transformation.

October 15

Compassion in Action

"Rejoice with those who rejoice; mourn with those who mourn."
Romans 12:15

DEVOTIONAL

Compassion often shines brightest in the everyday moments we share, inviting us to slow down and be fully present for those we love.

DAILY REFLECTION

What are some specific ways you can show compassion to someone in your life this week, and how might it make a difference? Consider the small, everyday actions that can create a ripple effect of kindness.

PRAYER

Dear God, help me to open my heart to those around me. May my actions reflect Your love and compassion in every encounter today.

Compassion is love in action, transforming the mundane into the miraculous.

October 16

The Power of a Quiet Yes

"A man has joy in giving an answer of his mouth, and a word spoken in due season, how good it is." **Proverbs 15:23**

DEVOTIONAL

Sometimes, our most powerful yes comes not from the rush to fill every role, but from the courage to prioritize our own well-being first.

DAILY REFLECTION

What does it mean for you to embrace the power of a quiet yes in your life today? How can you discern when to say yes, even in the midst of the chaos of motherhood and daily responsibilities?

PRAYER

Dear God, thank You for the moments of stillness amidst the busyness. Help me to listen for Your guiding voice and to give my heart and mind the grace to respond with a quiet yes, trusting in Your perfect plan.

In the silence of your heart, decisions become clearer, and peace finds its place.

October 17

Celebrating God's Goodness

"Give thanks to the Lord, for He is good; His love endures forever."
1 Chronicles 16:34

DEVOTIONAL

No matter how complex life becomes, remember to pause, reflect, and celebrate the goodness that surrounds you each day.

DAILY REFLECTION

What blessings in your life today remind you of God's goodness? How can you celebrate these moments, both big and small?

PRAYER

Dear Lord, thank you for your constant presence and unwavering goodness in my life. Help me to recognize and celebrate the blessings you provide each day with a grateful heart. Amen.

Every moment of gratitude opens the door to God's goodness.

October 18

Your Voice Matters

"Speak up for those who cannot speak for themselves; ensure justice for those being crushed. Yes, speak up for the poor and helpless, and see that they get justice." **Proverbs 31:8-9**

DEVOTIONAL

Your voice matters deeply, not just for you but for everyone around you. Whether it's comforting your child, advocating for a friend, or sharing your story, remember that speaking up can change lives.

DAILY REFLECTION

What unique experiences and insights do you possess that could uplift and inspire those around you?

PRAYER

Dear God, thank you for the gift of voice. Help me to recognize its power and to use it courageously to speak truth and love into the lives of others.

Your voice has the power to heal, guide, and transform those around you.

October 19

He Delights in You

*"The Lord your God is with you, the Mighty Warrior who saves. He will take great delight in you; in his love, he will no longer rebuke you, but will rejoice over you with singing." **Zephaniah 3:17***

DEVOTIONAL

You are a beloved creation, and your life brings joy to the heart of God.

DAILY REFLECTION

What are the ways you can intentionally recognize and embrace the delight that God takes in you, even amidst the chaos of daily life?

PRAYER

Dear Lord, thank You for the beautiful truth that You delight in me. Help me to open my heart to receive Your love and to walk each day with the assurance that I am cherished as Your daughter.

Your worth is not measured by your to-do list, but by the love that shapes your heart.

October 20

Pursuing God Over Perfection

"Set your minds on things that are above, not on things that are on earth."
Colossians 3:2

DEVOTIONAL

The pursuit of God allows us to embrace our messy, beautiful lives, reminding us that our worth isn't defined by our perfection but by our faith and love.

DAILY REFLECTION

What area of your life are you striving for perfection, and how might that be keeping you from a deeper connection with God? Reflect on this and consider what God wants to teach you in that space.

PRAYER

Dear Lord, help me to embrace my imperfections and seek Your presence in my everyday life. Guide me to find peace in Your love rather than in my accomplishments. Thank you for being the constant source of grace and strength.

Perfection is an illusion; grace is our reality.

October 21

Brave Steps of Obedience

"For with God, nothing will be impossible."
Luke 1:37

DEVOTIONAL

Embracing brave steps of obedience can reveal unexpected blessings and Every act of obedience, no matter how small, can lead to incredible transformations in your life and the lives of others.

DAILY REFLECTION

What brave step of obedience is God calling you to take right now in your life? Can you identify the fears or doubts that hold you back?

PRAYER

Dear Lord, thank You for Your guidance and strength as I navigate the challenges of motherhood and life. Help me to trust You more and take the brave steps You lay before me, knowing that You walk beside me every step of the way.

Obedience is the bridge that connects our fear to our faith.

October 22

Faith that Overflows

"But out of the abundance of the heart, the mouth speaks."
Luke 6:45

DEVOTIONAL

In the tumult of motherhood, remember that your faith is a well that can nourish not just you but those you love.

DAILY REFLECTION

What are the moments in your life when your faith has overflowed, and how can you cultivate those experiences to share with others?

PRAYER

Dear God, thank You for the gift of faith that sustains us. Help me to nurture an overflowing faith that not only supports me but also serves as a blessing to those around me. Amen.

Faith that overflows is not just a personal journey;
it's a shared river that nourishes the souls of others.

October 23

Finding Comfort in Scripture

"The Lord is close to the brokenhearted and saves those who are crushed in spirit." **Psalm 34:18**

DEVOTIONAL

In moments of struggle, remember that God's love surrounds you and His comfort awaits.

DAILY REFLECTION

What scripture has brought you comfort in challenging times, and how can you remind yourself of its truth today?

PRAYER

Dear God, thank you for your loving presence in my life. Help me to open my heart to your word and find solace in the promises you offer through scripture.

Your soul finds rest in the pages of His Word.

October 24

Strength for the Surrender

"Call to me and I will answer you, and show you great and mighty things, which you do not know." **Jeremiah 33:3**

DEVOTIONAL

In surrendering our burdens, we open ourselves to receive the strength and clarity we need for life's journey.

DAILY REFLECTION

What is one area in your life right now where you find it difficult to let go and surrender to God's plan? How might embracing surrender bring you strength and peace?

PRAYER

Dear God, thank You for being our constant source of strength. Help me to trust You more each day and to surrender my worries and fears into Your loving hands.

True strength often lies in the courage to let go and trust in a greater plan.

October 25

You Were Made for This Season

"Consider it pure joy, my sisters, whenever you face trials of many kinds, because you know that the testing of your faith produces perseverance."
James 1:2-3

DEVOTIONAL

In each of life's beautifully messy seasons, remember that every trial, every joy, and every moment prepares you for what is to come.

DAILY REFLECTION

What unique gifts and experiences has God given you that equip you for this season of your life? How can you lean into those strengths today?

PRAYER

Dear God, thank you for this beautiful season of life. Help me embrace the changes and challenges with grace, knowing that I am perfectly placed in Your plan.

You were made for this season,
not by accident but by intentional design.

October 26

The Anchor of God's Word

"For we live by faith, not by sight."
2 Corinthians 5:7

DEVOTIONAL

The storms of life may be fierce, yet a steadfast reliance on God's Word provides the focus and strength we need to navigate through any challenge.

DAILY REFLECTION

What verses or promises from God's Word have anchored you during challenging seasons in your life? How can you intentionally hold onto those truths today?

PRAYER

Dear Lord, thank you for the gift of Your Word, a steadfast anchor in our lives. Help us to lean into its wisdom and find solace as we navigate each day with grace and clarity.

In times of storm, His promises become our safe harbor.

October 27

Trusting Him, Even in Silence

"Be still, and know that I am God."
Psalm 46:10

DEVOTIONAL

The lesson here is that even when you feel unheard, take comfort in knowing that in those silent moments, God is working behind the scenes, preparing something beautiful for you.

DAILY REFLECTION

What does it look like for you to trust God during the quiet moments of your life, especially when answers seem distant or silence prevails? How can you embrace this season of waiting with a heart open to His wisdom?

PRAYER

Dear God, thank You for being present with us, even in the silence. Help us to trust Your perfect timing and find peace in knowing that You are working behind the scenes.

Silence does not mean absence: it often signifies preparation for something beautiful ahead.

October 28

Living Gratefully

"I have learned to be content whatever the circumstances. I know what it is to be in need, and I know what it is to have plenty. I have learned the secret of being content in any and every situation... I can do all this through Him who gives me strength." **Philippians 4:11-13**

DEVOTIONAL

Gratitude transforms our perspective, helping us to see the rich tapestry of blessings woven into our daily lives, even amidst the imperfections.

DAILY REFLECTION

What are three things in your life right now that you can choose to view through the lens of gratitude, even if they come with challenges? Consider how these aspects might shape your perspective.

PRAYER

Dear God, thank You for the blessings that surround me, even in the mundane. Help me to embrace a heart of gratitude, finding joy in the simple gifts of each day.

Gratitude turns what we have into enough.

October 29

Your Story Reflects His Glory

"And we know that in all things God works for the good of those who love him, who have been called according to his purpose." **Romans 8:28**

DEVOTIONAL

The beauty of your everyday life can be a canvas that displays God's glory, even in the seemingly mundane moments.

DAILY REFLECTION

What moments in your life have showcased God's grace and faithfulness, and how can you share those stories to inspire others?

PRAYER

Dear Lord, thank You for the unique story You are weaving in my life. Help me to see Your glory reflected in my journey and to share that light with those around me. Amen.

Every chapter of your life tells a story of God's glory unveiled through your experiences.

October 30

Walking in the Light

"But if we walk in the light, as He is in the light, we have fellowship with one another, and the blood of Jesus His Son cleanses us from all sin." **1 John 1:7**

DEVOTIONAL

Remember, dear sister, that in the gentle embrace of light, you will find clarity amidst chaos and joy woven into the fabric of your daily life.

DAILY REFLECTION

What does it mean for you to walk in the light during this season of your life? How can embracing this path transform your role as a mom and illuminate your relationships?

PRAYER

Dear God, thank You for being the light in our lives. Help me to walk in Your light daily, guiding my heart and my actions as I navigate motherhood and beyond.

Walking in the light means choosing clarity over confusion, hope over despair, and connection over isolation.

October 31

Gratitude in Every Circumstance

"Give thanks in all circumstances; for this is God's will for you in Christ Jesus." **1 Thessalonians 5:18**

DEVOTIONAL

In every moment, even those filled with challenges, choose gratitude as a powerful lens through which to view your life.

DAILY REFLECTION

What circumstances in your life today can you intentionally choose to be grateful for, even if they seem challenging?

PRAYER

Dear God, thank you for the gift of life and the opportunities to grow through every experience. Help me to embrace gratitude in every situation, trusting that Your plans are always for my good.

"Gratitude transforms ordinary moments into extraordinary blessings.

November 1

He is Faithful Still

"The one who calls you is faithful, and he will do it."
1 Thessalonians 5:24

DEVOTIONAL

He is faithful still, even when your heart feels heavy.

DAILY REFLECTION

What situations in your life remind you of God's unwavering faithfulness, even in difficult times? How can you lean into that faithfulness today?

PRAYER

Dear God, thank you for your constant presence in our lives. Help us to trust in your faithfulness as we navigate our days, knowing that you are with us in every moment.

In every season of life. His faithfulness overflows like a gentle river. guiding us through uncertainty and doubt.

November 2

Strength in Surrender

Hebrews 4:15-16 *reminds us that we have a High Priest who understands our struggles. In moments of fear or doubt, let us approach the throne of grace with confidence, knowing we will receive mercy and find grace to help us in our time of need*

DEVOTIONAL

Surrendering to God's plan can transform our worries into opportunities for growth and connection.

DAILY REFLECTION

What does it look like for you to surrender your worries and fears to God in this season of your life, and what strength might you find in that act of letting go?

PRAYER

Dear God, teach me the beauty of surrender. Help me to release my burdens into Your hands, trusting in Your strength and perfect plan for my life.

In surrendering. we find the freedom to embrace what truly matters.

November 3

The Power of Remembering

"I will remember the deeds of the Lord; yes, I will remember your miracles of long ago. I will consider all your works and meditate on all your mighty deeds." Psalm 77:11-12

DEVOTIONAL

Life's challenges often fade away in the light of the memories we cherish.

DAILY REFLECTION

What moments from your past have shaped you most profoundly, and how can revisiting them inspire your present journey as a mother and a woman?

PRAYER

Dear God, thank you for the gift of memory. Help me to cherish the lessons from my past and embrace them as a source of strength. Guide my thoughts as I reflect on Your faithfulness through the years.

Remembering can be a sacred act.
bridging the past and present with grace and gratitude.

November 4

Walking Through Grief with God

"The righteous person may have many troubles, but the Lord delivers him from them all." Psalm 34:19

DEVOTIONAL

In the midst of grief, it's okay to pause, to feel, and to allow yourself to navigate the waves of emotion with God by your side.

DAILY REFLECTION

What memories of lost loved ones do you cherish the most, and how can you invite God into those moments of remembrance?

PRAYER

Dear God, in this time of sorrow, help me to feel Your presence beside me. Wrap me in Your love as I navigate through the waves of grief and loss.

Grief is not only a journey of sorrow
but also an avenue to deeper intimacy with God.

November 5

Rest for the Weary

Matthew 6:31-33 reminds us not to worry about our needs but to seek first the kingdom of God and His righteousness. As we shift our focus, we find that His provision meets us in the most unexpected ways, often when we feel we have nothing left to give.

DEVOTIONAL

In moments of weariness, remember that your worth is not tied to your productivity, but to the love and grace you give freely.

DAILY REFLECTION

What do you do to find rest amidst the busyness of your life, and how can you intentionally carve out moments of peace for yourself today?

PRAYER

Dear God, thank You for being a refuge for our weary hearts. Please help me to embrace the rest You offer and to prioritize moments of stillness in my hectic schedule.

Rest is not merely the absence of work; it is the presence of peace.

November 6

Finding Contentment in Christ

"Every good gift and perfect gift is from above, coming down from the Father of lights." **James 1:17**

DEVOTIONAL

In the pursuit of contentment, it's essential to recognize and embrace the beauty in every ordinary moment that life offers.

DAILY REFLECTION

What are the areas in your life where you struggle to find contentment, and how might surrendering those concerns to Christ bring you peace?

PRAYER

Dear Lord, guide me to recognize the true source of my joy and help me surrender my worries to You. Fill my heart with Your peace and a sense of fulfillment in each moment.

Contentment is not the absence of desire but the presence of Christ in the midst of our longing.

November 7

You Are Held

*"Come to me, all you who are weary and burdened, and I will give you rest. Take my yoke upon you and learn from me, for I am gentle and humble in heart, and you will find rest for your souls." **Matthew 11:28-29***

DEVOTIONAL

You have the strength to face the challenges of motherhood, knowing that you are tenderly held and supported in all aspects of your life.

DAILY REFLECTION

What areas in your life do you feel burdened or uncertain right now, and how might recognizing that you're held in God's embrace change your perspective?

PRAYER

Dear Lord, thank you for the reminder that we are held in Your loving embrace. Help us to find comfort and strength in Your presence today as we navigate the challenges of motherhood and life.

You are held, cherished beyond measure, and grounded in love.

November 8

A Spirit of Thanksgiving

"Give thanks to the Lord, for He is good; His love endures forever."
Psalm 107:1

DEVOTIONAL

Find gratitude in the small moments, for they often carry the greatest blessings of all.

DAILY REFLECTION

What are the small moments in your day that spark gratitude, even amid life's challenges? How can you cultivate a spirit of thanksgiving in those everyday experiences?

PRAYER

Dear God, thank you for this moment to reflect on the blessings in my life. Help me to recognize the beauty in each day and to share that gratitude with others.

Thankfulness turns what we have into enough and more.

November 9

When God Feels Distant

"The Lord is near to all who call on Him, to all who call on Him in truth."
Psalm 145:18

DEVOTIONAL

Even in our busiest moments and deepest struggles, God is always just a whisper away, inviting us to reach out and reconnect with Him.

DAILY REFLECTION

What are the moments in your life when you've felt God's presence slip away, and how can you invite Him back into those spaces now?

PRAYER

Dear Lord, in moments of silence and distance, remind us that You are always close, even when we feel alone. Help us to seek You with open hearts and to find comfort in Your unwavering love.

Even in the quiet, God is whispering His presence.

November 10

Peace That Passes Understanding

Philippians 4:7 *reminds us that the peace of God, which transcends all understanding, will guard our hearts and minds in Christ Jesus. Embrace this divine tranquility, dear mom, as you navigate the beautiful yet tumultuous journey of motherhood and life.*

DEVOTIONAL

True peace comes when we release our burdens to God, knowing He is in control of every situation we face.

DAILY REFLECTION

What are the situations in your life that challenge your peace, and how can you invite God into those moments today?

PRAYER

Dear Lord, help me to find rest in Your presence and trust that You are in control. Fill my heart with Your peace that transcends all understanding, today and every day.

Peace is not the absence of trouble, but the assurance of His presence.

November 11

He Restores What Was Broken

"Create in me a clean heart, O God, and renew a right spirit within me."
Psalm 51:10

DEVOTIONAL

In recognizing and addressing our struggles, we create space for God to restore the brokenness in our lives.

DAILY REFLECTION

What areas in your life feel broken or in need of restoration? How can you invite God into those spaces for healing and renewal?

PRAYER

Dear Lord, thank You for the promise that You restore what has been broken in our lives. Help me to trust in Your healing power and open my heart to the beautiful transformation You desire for me.

Out of the ashes. He brings forth beauty.

November 12

You Are Called and Equipped

"It is He who goes before you. He will be with you; He will not leave you or forsake you. Do not fear or be dismayed." **Deuteronomy 31:8**

DEVOTIONAL

Trust that you are uniquely called and divinely equipped for this season of your life, with strengths and wisdom you have gained along the way.

DAILY REFLECTION

What unique gifts and strengths do you possess that can make a difference in your family and community? Reflect on how God has uniquely equipped you for this season of your life.

PRAYER

Dear God, thank you for the beautiful call on my life. Help me to recognize the gifts you've placed within me and to use them boldly for Your glory.

Your calling is woven into the very fabric of your being; embrace it with confidence.

November 13

Hope That Anchors

"To them God has chosen to make known among the Gentiles the glorious riches of this mystery, which is Christ in you, the hope of glory."
Colossians 1:27

DEVOTIONAL

In the ever-shifting landscape of motherhood, remember that the hope you hold can illuminate the paths of both your life and your family's journey.

DAILY REFLECTION

What anchors your hope in the midst of life's storms? Can you identify moments when that hope has held you steady?

PRAYER

Dear God, thank you for being our anchor amid life's ebb and flow. May we find strength and peace in Your promises, and may our hearts be filled with hope that never fades.

Hope is the gentle whisper that reminds us we're not alone in our journey.

November 14

A Grateful Heart is a Strong Heart

"Enter his gates with thanksgiving and his courts with praise; give thanks to him and praise his name." **Psalm 100:4**

DEVOTIONAL

Gratitude is not just a feeling; it's a powerful choice that can transform chaos into calm and strengthen us amidst life's challenges.

DAILY REFLECTION

What are the moments in your life that have filled you with gratitude, and how can you embrace those feelings to strengthen your heart and spirit today?

PRAYER

Dear God, thank You for the many blessings and lessons in our lives. Help us to cultivate a heart full of gratitude, recognizing the strength that comes from appreciating both the joys and challenges we face.

A grateful heart radiates strength and resilience, empowering us to navigate life's storms with grace.

November 15

Letting Go of What No Longer Serves

"The Lord had said to Abram, 'Go from your country, your people, and your father's household to the land I will show you." **Genesis 12:1**

DEVOTIONAL

Letting go of what no longer serves us opens up space for new blessings and opportunities that align with our purpose.

DAILY REFLECTION

What are the beliefs, habits, or relationships in your life that are holding you back from embracing your fullest self?

PRAYER

Dear Lord, help me to recognize what no longer serves me and give me the courage to let go. Fill my heart with peace as I release the burdens that weigh me down, trusting in Your guidance for the path ahead.

Letting go is not an end; it is the beginning of a new chapter of growth and renewal.

November 16

Faith in the Fire

"I will bring that group through the fire and make them pure; I will refine them like silver and test them like gold. They will call on my name, and I will answer them; I will say, 'They are my people,' and they will say, 'The Lord is our God." **Zechariah 13:9**

DEVOTIONAL

When faith meets the flames of life's challenges, it not only survives but emerges stronger and more vibrant than before.

DAILY REFLECTION

What are the fires in your life that challenge your faith, and how can you embrace them as an opportunity for growth?

PRAYER

Dear God, as we journey through life's trials, help us to see Your presence in the flames. Strengthen our hearts and renew our spirits, guiding us through the heat with grace and hope.

Faith is not the absence of fire but the assurance that we will emerge refined.

November 17

The Blessing of Today

"This is the day that the Lord has made; let us rejoice and be glad in it."
Psalm 118:24

DEVOTIONAL

Every day carries its unique blessings, urging us to pause, breathe, and celebrate the small joys life unfolds before us.

DAILY REFLECTION

What small blessings have you noticed in your life today, and how do they reflect God's love for you?

PRAYER

Dear Lord, thank you for the gift of today and the blessings it brings. Help me to embrace each moment with gratitude and to recognize Your hand at work in my life.

Today is a canvas; paint it with the colors of gratitude and joy.

November 18

Preparing Your Heart for Worship

"Come, let us bow down in worship, let us kneel before the Lord our Maker; for He is our God and we are the people of His pasture, the flock under His care." **Psalm 95:6-7**

DEVOTIONAL

To cultivate a heart for worship, we must intentionally carve out moments of peace and reflection amidst our busy lives.

DAILY REFLECTION

What distractions may be stealing your focus from God this week, and how can you intentionally set them aside as you prepare your heart for worship?

PRAYER

Heavenly Father, help me to quiet my heart and ears to hear You above the noise of daily life. May Your peace envelop me as I come before You in worship.

Worship is not just an act,
but a readiness of the heart to encounter the divine.

November 19

Trust That Triumphs

"Many sorrows surround the wicked, but steadfast love surrounds the one who trusts in the Lord." **Psalm 32:10**

DEVOTIONAL

Trust in the journey, knowing that a heart anchored in faith can overcome life's storms.

DAILY REFLECTION

What situations in your life are calling for greater trust in God's plan? How might surrendering to Him lead to unexpected triumphs?

PRAYER

Dear God, thank You for being our constant source of strength and assurance. Help us to lean on You in times of uncertainty, trusting that You have a perfect plan for our lives.

Trust takes the first step even when the path isn't clear.

November 20

Thankfulness as Worship

"And let the peace that comes from Christ rule in your hearts. For as members of one body, you are called to live in peace and always be thankful." **Colossians 3:15**

DEVOTIONAL

Every act of thankfulness in your life is an act of worship that brings you closer to God's peace and purpose.

DAILY REFLECTION

What are the small, everyday moments in your life that you can turn into acts of gratitude and worship? How can you invite God's presence into these moments?

PRAYER

Dear Lord, thank you for the countless blessings you weave into the fabric of our daily lives. Help me to see each moment as an opportunity to express my thankfulness and deeper devotion to you.

Thankfulness is not just a response;
it is an invitation to encounter the divine in everyday life.

November 21

God's Goodness Never Fails

"For the Lord is good and his love endures forever; his faithfulness continues through all generations." **Psalm 100:5**

DEVOTIONAL

Even in the whirlwind of life's demands, remember that God's goodness is a constant, wrapping us in love and comfort through every season.

DAILY REFLECTION

What moment in your life have you struggled to see God's goodness, and how can reflecting on that experience help you trust Him more fully today?

PRAYER

Dear God, thank you for your steadfast goodness that surrounds us daily. Help me to open my heart to recognize and embrace your blessings, especially in moments of doubt. May I hold tight to your promises and find peace in your unwavering love.

Even in seasons of uncertainty,
God's goodness is a constant companion.

November 22

Celebrating Small Things

"Rejoice always, pray continually, give thanks in all circumstances; for this is God's will for you in Christ Jesus." **1 Thessalonians 5:16-18**

DEVOTIONAL

It's often the little moments—like laughter over dinner or a spontaneous hug —that remind you to savor the beauty in each day.

DAILY REFLECTION

What small moments in your daily life bring you joy, and how can you celebrate them more intentionally?

PRAYER

Dear God, thank you for the beauty found in life's small moments. Help me to open my heart to appreciate and celebrate these gifts each day.

Every small joy is a stepping stone on the path to gratitude.

November 23

His Mercy Is New Today

"The steadfast love of the Lord never ceases; His mercies never come to an end; they are new every morning; great is Your faithfulness."
Lamentations 3:22-23

DEVOTIONAL

No matter what challenges you faced yesterday, remember that His mercy is a fresh gift for today, empowering you to embrace the newness of life.

DAILY REFLECTION

What burdens or regrets from yesterday are you carrying into today that you could lay down at His feet, trusting in His renewing mercy?

PRAYER

Loving God, thank You for the gift of today. Help me release my past and embrace the new mercies You've poured out for me this morning.

Every sunrise brings a fresh opportunity to experience His grace.

November 24

Rooted in Gratitude

"And let the peace of Christ rule in your hearts, to which indeed you were called in one body. And be thankful." **Colossians 3:15**

DEVOTIONAL

Gratitude shifts our focus from what we lack to the abundance that surrounds us, nurturing our hearts and bringing peace to our busy lives.

DAILY REFLECTION

What are three specific things in your life right now that you can choose to focus on with gratitude, even amidst the daily challenges? How can you intentionally bring those into your prayers and conversations this week?

PRAYER

Heavenly Father, thank You for the countless blessings in our lives, both big and small. Help us to cultivate a heart of gratitude amidst the busyness of motherhood and daily responsibilities. May we see Your hand in every moment.

Gratitude isn't just a feeling; it's a choice that transforms our perspective and nourishes our souls.

November 25

Overflowing with Thanksgiving

"Give thanks to the Lord, for he is good; his love endures forever."
1 Chronicles 16:34

DEVOTIONAL

Embrace the everyday blessings in your life, for within them, your heart will discover an abundance of gratitude that uplifts your spirit.

DAILY REFLECTION

What are the blessings in your life, both big and small, that bring you the most joy and how can you express gratitude for them today?

PRAYER

Dear God, thank you for the countless gifts you have placed in my life. Help me to recognize and appreciate your blessings, cultivating a heart that overflows with thanksgiving every day.

Gratitude transforms ordinary moments into extraordinary blessings.

November 26

God's Faithfulness Through Generations

"For I know that my Redeemer lives, and at the last he will stand upon the earth." **Job 19:25**

DEVOTIONAL

God's faithfulness is a precious inheritance we pass down to our children, teaching them that when faced with the challenges life presents, they can lean on the same truths that have sustained us.

DAILY REFLECTION

What examples of God's faithfulness have you witnessed in your life and the lives of those who came before you? How can you share these stories with your children to inspire their faith?

PRAYER

Dear Lord, thank you for the unwavering faithfulness you show across generations. Help me to recognize and celebrate the ways you've been present in my life and in my family. May I inspire others by sharing these truths.

God's faithfulness is the thread that weaves through the tapestry of our family history.

November 27

Blessed to Be a Blessing

"Let each of you look not only to his own interests, but also to the interests of others." **Philippians 2:4**

DEVOTIONAL

You are a vessel overflowing with love; as you invest in others, you enrich your own soul.

DAILY REFLECTION

What does it mean for you to recognize the blessings in your life, and how can you use those blessings to uplift others around you?

PRAYER

Heavenly Father, thank you for the gifts you have bestowed upon us. Help me to recognize the blessings in my life and inspire me to share them generously with those I encounter.

Every blessing you receive is an invitation to bless someone else.

November 28

Finding Joy in Simplicity

"And why do you worry about clothes? See how the flowers of the field grow. They do not labor or spin. Yet I tell you that not even Solomon in all his splendor was dressed like one of these." **Matthew 6:28-29**

DEVOTIONAL

Finding joy in simplicity means recognizing that true happiness often resides in the small, everyday wonders rather than the grand achievements of life.

DAILY REFLECTION

What small moments in your daily life bring you joy and remind you of what truly matters? How can you cultivate more of these experiences in your routine?

PRAYER

Dear Lord, thank you for the simple blessings that surround us each day. Help me to embrace these moments and find joy in the quiet spaces of my life.

Joy is found not in the grand events,
but in the gentle rhythm of everyday life.

November 29

Grace to End the Month Well

"Let us approach God's throne of grace with confidence, so that we may receive mercy and find grace to help us in our time of need."
Hebrews 4:16

DEVOTIONAL

Remember, as you end this month, that grace is not just a concept—it's an inviting embrace asking you to relinquish the pressure to be perfect and to stay tender toward yourself.

DAILY REFLECTION

What has this month taught you about God's grace, and how can you carry those lessons into the next month?

PRAYER

Dear God, thank you for your unfailing grace that carries us through every day. Help me to recognize and embrace this grace as I close this month, and inspire me to share it with those around me.

Grace transforms our endings into new beginnings.

November 30

Preparing Him Room

"And she gave birth to her firstborn, a son. She wrapped him in cloths and placed him in a manger because there was no guest room available for them." **Luke 2:7**

DEVOTIONAL

Let us intentionally prepare room in our hearts for Jesus amidst our busy days, allowing Him to be the true focus of our lives and celebrations.

DAILY REFLECTION

What does it mean for you to truly prepare room in your heart and home for the love and presence of those you cherish? How can you create space for joy and connection amidst the busyness of life?

PRAYER

Dear Lord, help me to clear out the clutter that fills my heart and my home. Teach me to create sacred space where love can flourish and your presence can dwell.

To prepare Him room is to embrace the quiet moments and fill them with love and intention.

December 1

Peace in the Waiting

"For I, the Lord your God, hold your right hand; it is I who say to you, 'Fear not, I am the one who helps you.'" **Isaiah 41:13**

DEVOTIONAL

The lesson here is that in our waiting, peace can be found by leaning into faith, knowing that God is present in every step of our journey.

DAILY REFLECTION

What areas of your life are you currently waiting on, and how might you cultivate peace in that process?

PRAYER

Dear God, in moments of waiting, help me to find solace in your presence. Grant me the patience to trust your timing and the strength to embrace the journey ahead.

Peace isn't found in the resolution of waiting but in the assurance that you are never alone.

December 2

The Gift of Hope

"May the God of hope fill you with all joy and peace as you trust in Him, so that you may overflow with hope by the power of the Holy Spirit."
Romans 15:13

DEVOTIONAL

As a woman navigating the complexities of life, remember that hope is your anchor; it is the quiet strength that can guide you through the storms of motherhood and beyond.

DAILY REFLECTION

What hopes and dreams have you tucked away, and how might you bring them back to the surface in your life today?

PRAYER

Dear Lord, thank you for the promise of hope in every season of life. Help me to embrace the dreams you've planted in my heart and give me courage to nurture them.

Hope is not just a feeling; it is a choice we make every day to believe in a brighter future.

December 3

Emmanuel—God With Us

"The virgin will conceive and give birth to a son, and they will call him Immanuel, which means 'God with us.'" **Matthew 1:23**

DEVOTIONAL

No matter how overwhelming life may feel, God is always by our side, offering us strength, love, and comfort through every moment.

DAILY REFLECTION

What does it mean for you to invite God into the everyday moments of your life as a mom? How might acknowledging His presence transform your experiences?

PRAYER

Dear God, thank You for being with us in every moment of our lives. Help us to feel Your presence more profoundly in our daily routines, bringing peace as we navigate our roles as mothers and caregivers.

Emmanuel—God with us—
reminds us that we are never alone in our journey.

December 4

Letting God Interrupt Your Plans

"In their hearts humans plan their course,
but the Lord establishes their steps." **Proverbs 16:9**

DEVOTIONAL

Sometimes, the interruptions in our meticulously crafted lives are God's way of drawing us closer to what truly matters.

DAILY REFLECTION

What plans are you holding tightly to that might need a little room for divine interruption? Can you think of a time when letting go of your agenda led to something beautiful and unexpected?

PRAYER

Dear God, help me to embrace the twists and turns of life with open arms. May I find peace in your perfect timing as I navigate my plans and trust in your greater purpose.

Sometimes, the detours are the very paths we are meant to follow.

December 5

The Light Has Come

"The light shines in the darkness, and the darkness has not overcome it."
John 1:5

DEVOTIONAL
Embrace the light that has come into your life; even in the chaos, it's there to guide you through every trial.

DAILY REFLECTION
What areas of your life are you waiting for the light of hope to shine through right now? How can you seek that light in your daily challenges?

PRAYER
Dear God, thank you for being a constant source of light in our lives. Help me to embrace your warmth and guidance, especially in the moments when I feel lost or overwhelmed.

*In the moments of darkness, remember that
the light is never far away; it is within you and all around you.*

December 6

He Fulfills His Promises

"Let us hold unswervingly to the hope we profess, for he who promised is faithful." **Hebrews 10:23**

DEVOTIONAL
When life feels heavy, trust that God is faithful to fulfill His promises, just as you fulfill yours for those you love.

DAILY REFLECTION
What promises has God made to you that you are still waiting to see fulfilled in your life? How can you find peace and strength in His timing as you reflect on these promises today?

PRAYER
Dear Lord, thank You for Your faithfulness and the promises You've made to us. Help me to trust in Your perfect timing, finding comfort in knowing that You always fulfill what You have spoken. Amen.

*His promises are not bound by time;
they unfold beautifully in the tapestry of our lives.*

December 7

A Season of Surrender

"Truly my soul finds rest in God; my salvation comes from him. Truly he is my rock and my salvation; he is my fortress, I will never be shaken."
Psalm 62:1-2

DEVOTIONAL

Sometimes, surrendering doesn't mean giving up; it means allowing God to take over and find peace in the chaos of life.

DAILY REFLECTION

What burdens are you holding onto that might need to be released into God's loving hands? Consider how surrendering these can lead to deeper peace and joy in your life.

PRAYER

Dear Lord, help me to trust in Your perfect timing and to gently release my worries to You. May Your guidance fill my heart as I embrace this season of surrender.

Surrendering is not giving up: it's letting go
of the illusion of control and allowing grace to fill the gaps.

December 8

Welcoming Wonder

"This is the day that the Lord has made; let us rejoice and be glad in it."
Psalm 118:24

DEVOTIONAL

Embracing the wonders in our lives invites joy and gratitude, helping us reconnect with the present moment.

DAILY REFLECTION

What small wonders have you overlooked in your daily life that could spark joy or gratitude today? How might you take a moment to pause and truly welcome them?

PRAYER

Dear God, thank You for the everyday wonders that surround us. Help me to open my heart to see and cherish the blessings within the chaos of motherhood and life.

In the midst of our busy lives, wonder waits quietly to be noticed.

December 9

Trusting Through Transition

"Commit your way to the Lord; trust in Him and He will act."
Psalm 37:5

DEVOTIONAL

In each season of change, trusting God transforms what feels like uncertainty into a pathway for growth.

DAILY REFLECTION

What transitions are you currently facing, and how can you lean into God's guidance during this time?

PRAYER

Dear God, thank You for being our constant companion through every change in life. Help us to trust You, embracing the new paths ahead with confidence and grace. May we find peace in Your presence as we navigate these transitions.

Trust is a journey, not a destination;
it's about taking each step with faith despite the unknown.

December 10

The Strength of a Willing Heart

"Blessed is the one who trusts in the Lord, whose confidence is in him. They will be like a tree planted by the water that sends out its roots by the stream. It does not fear when heat comes; its leaves are always green. It has no worries in a year of drought and never fails to bear fruit."
Jeremiah 17:7-8

DEVOTIONAL

A willing heart, anchored in faith, creates resilience to face the challenges of motherhood and life.

DAILY REFLECTION

What is one area in your life where you feel God is inviting you to step out in faith with a willing heart? How can you embrace His call with joy and courage?

PRAYER

Dear God, thank You for the gift of a willing heart. Help me to find strength in my willingness to serve and love others, and remind me of the impact I can have when I step forward in faith.

A willing heart opens the door to endless possibilities.

December 11

Heaven's Perspective

"I lift up my eyes to the hills—where does my help come from? My help comes from the Lord, the Maker of heaven and earth." **Psalm 121:1-2**

DEVOTIONAL

Life can throw challenges that feel too heavy to bear, but when we adopt Heaven's perspective, we can see our trials through the lens of hope and purpose.

DAILY REFLECTION

What does it mean for you to see your life through Heaven's perspective, especially in the midst of daily challenges and responsibilities?

PRAYER

Dear God, help me to lift my gaze toward You today. Let Your perspective fill my heart with peace and purpose, reminding me of the eternity I am promised.

Viewing our lives through Heaven's lens encourages us to cherish the present while staying anchored in hope.

December 12

Finding Joy in Christ

"I will greatly rejoice in the Lord; my soul shall exult in my God, for he has clothed me with the garments of salvation; he has covered me with the robe of righteousness..." **Isaiah 61:10**

DEVOTIONAL

Finding joy in Christ isn't about the absence of challenges; it's about recognizing His presence in the midst of our daily lives. When we slow down and shift our focus from our burdens to His promises, we can unearth the joy that has been with us all along—woven into the fabric of our everyday moments.

DAILY REFLECTION

What are the little moments in your day where you can pause and invite Christ into your heart, allowing His joy to wash over you?

PRAYER

Dear Lord, thank You for the gift of Your presence in our lives. Help me to embrace the joy You offer and to share it with my family and those around me each day.

Joy is not the absence of challenges, but the presence of Christ in all circumstances.

December 13

Holding Space for Silence

"Yes, my soul, find rest in God; my hope comes from him. Truly he is my rock and my salvation; he is my fortress, I will not be shaken."
Psalm 62:5-6

DEVOTIONAL

Creating space for silence allows us to reconnect with our true selves and recognize our own needs amidst the busyness of life.

DAILY REFLECTION

What does holding space for silence mean to you in this hectic season of life, and how can it transform your relationship with yourself and your loved ones?

PRAYER

Dear God, as I seek moments of quiet amidst the busyness, allow me to feel your comforting presence and embrace the silence that nourishes my spirit. Help me find peace in these still moments, where I can hear your guidance.

Silence is not the absence of sound, but the presence of peace.

December 14

Receiving God's Peace

"And the peace of God, which transcends all understanding, will guard your hearts and your minds in Christ Jesus." **Philippians 4:7**

DEVOTIONAL

Embrace the quiet moments, for within them lies the peace of God waiting to guard your heart.

DAILY REFLECTION

What does it feel like to you when you truly embrace the peace of God in your busy life? Can you recall a moment where His tranquility washed over you, providing solace amidst chaos?

PRAYER

Dear God, thank You for the gift of peace that surpasses all understanding. Help me to quiet my heart and mind, allowing Your presence to fill me with comfort and assurance.

God's peace is an anchor for the soul in the storms of life.

December 15

An Invitation to Stillness

"Be still, and know that I am God."
Psalm 46:10

DEVOTIONAL

In the stillness of life's chaos, we can rediscover the peace and strength that comes from knowing God is always with us.

DAILY REFLECTION

What does stillness mean to you, and how can you carve out a few moments of quiet in your busy life to reconnect with your inner self and God?

PRAYER

Dear Lord, help me find peace in the midst of my daily chaos. Teach me to embrace stillness, allowing Your presence to fill my heart and guide my thoughts. Amen.

Stillness isn't a void; it's a space
where God can meet us in our hearts.

December 16

The Heart of Generosity

"Each of you should give what you have decided in your heart to give, not reluctantly or under compulsion, for God loves a cheerful giver."
2 Corinthians 9:7

DEVOTIONAL

In every act of kindness, no matter how small, lies the potential to enrich not only the lives of others but our own as well.

DAILY REFLECTION

What does generosity look like in the everyday moments of your life, and how can you cultivate it in surprising ways with your family and friends? Reflect on how small acts of kindness can create a ripple effect in your community.

PRAYER

Dear Lord, thank You for the many blessings in our lives. Help us to share these gifts with generous hearts, making a difference in the lives of those around us. May our actions reflect Your love and kindness each day.

Generosity is not just about giving; it's about
creating a culture of kindness that inspires others.

Near the End of Our Journey

You have spent many days reflecting through these devotionals.

If this book has supported your spiritual journey, sharing a short review on Amazon helps more women discover these pages of encouragement.

devo.anchoredgraces.com/2026

Your story may be the reason another woman finds hope.

December 17

God's Perfect Timing

"And we know that in all things God works for the good of those who love him, who have been called according to his purpose." **Romans 8:28**

DEVOTIONAL

Trust that the moments you feel most uncertain are often the moments that God is preparing you for something extraordinary.

DAILY REFLECTION

What areas of your life are you struggling to understand God's timing? How might surrendering those feelings open your heart to His plans?

PRAYER

Dear Lord, thank You for always knowing what is best for us. Help me to trust Your perfect timing in my life, even when I can't see the path ahead.

Trusting in God's perfect timing allows us to find peace in every season.

December 18

Resting in His Goodness

"Surely your goodness and love will follow me all the days of my life, and I will dwell in the house of the Lord forever." **Psalm 23:6**

DEVOTIONAL

God's goodness is always with you, reminding you to pause and rest amidst your responsibilities, knowing that you are enveloped in His love.

DAILY REFLECTION

What areas of your life do you find it most difficult to trust in His goodness? Can you identify moments when His faithfulness has shown up, even amidst uncertainty?

PRAYER

Dear Lord, help me to rest in Your goodness, even when life's challenges seem overwhelming. May I be continually reminded of Your faithfulness and love in my daily journey. Amen.

His goodness is a soft blanket on a chilly night, offering warmth and comfort to our weary souls.

December 19

He Came for You

"But God demonstrates His own love for us in this: While we were still sinners, Christ died for us." **Romans 5:8**

DEVOTIONAL

You are deeply loved and valued, simply for being you, not for what you accomplish.

DAILY REFLECTION

What does it mean to you that Jesus came specifically for you, in all your uniqueness and imperfections? How can you embrace His love in your everyday life?

PRAYER

Dear Lord, thank You for coming into my life, just as I am. Help me to rest in the knowledge that Your love is unconditional and always surrounds me.

He came for you, not for the perfect version of yourself, but for the real you, filled with hopes, dreams, and struggles.

December 20

Awe and Adoration

"O Lord, our Lord, how majestic is your name in all the earth! You have set your glory above the heavens." **Psalm 8:1**

DEVOTIONAL

God's grandeur surrounds us, even amidst the ordinary chaos of motherhood; it's our choice to take a moment to breathe and be still, allowing awe and adoration to fill our hearts.

DAILY REFLECTION

What moments have taken your breath away lately, inviting you to pause and reflect on the beauty around you?

PRAYER

Dear God, thank you for the wonders of the world and the blessings in my life. Help me to pause in awe and let my heart overflow in adoration for all that you have created.

In the stillness of your heart, find the extraordinary in the ordinary.

December 21

Grace for the Holidays

"For by grace you have been saved through faith, and that not of yourselves; it is the gift of God, not of works, lest anyone should boast."
Ephesians 2:8-9

DEVOTIONAL

As we embrace the holidays, remember that grace isn't just for the perfect moments; it's even more beautiful in our messy, imperfect ones.

DAILY REFLECTION

What does grace look like for you during the holiday season, especially when tensions run high and expectations seem overwhelming? How can you extend that same grace to those around you, including yourself?

PRAYER

Dear God, thank you for the gift of grace that brings peace to our hearts, especially during the busy holiday season. Help me to embrace that grace and share it with my family and friends. May I find joy in the moments and strength in your love.

Grace transforms the chaos of the holidays into a tapestry of love and joy.

December 22

Wrapped in His Love

"For I am convinced that neither death nor life, neither angels nor demons, neither the present nor the future, nor any powers, neither height nor depth, nor anything else in all creation will be able to separate us from the love of God." **Romans 8:38-39**

DEVOTIONAL

3. Life Lesson: In the whirlwind of daily life, remember that you are wrapped in God's unwavering love, which gives you the strength to embrace each moment.

DAILY REFLECTION

What are the ways you have experienced God's love wrapping around you during challenging moments of your journey?

PRAYER

Dear Lord, thank you for enveloping me in Your love each day. Help me to be aware of Your presence and to reflect that love to my family and those around me.

In every moment of doubt, remember that your worth s defined by His love, not your circumstances.

December 23

A Holy Night

*"For to us a child is born, to us a son is given; and the government shall be upon his shoulder, and his name shall be called Wonderful Counselor, Mighty God, Everlasting Father, Prince of Peace." **Isaiah 9:6***

DEVOTIONAL

In the flurry of life, make space for holy moments that refresh your spirit and reaffirm your purpose.

DAILY REFLECTION

What does a "holy night" look like in your life, and how can you create moments of peace and joy amidst the busyness?

PRAYER

Dear God, help me find your presence in the quiet moments of my life. May I embrace your peace and love tonight, knowing you are with me, guiding my heart and thoughts.

Every night holds the potential for divine connection if we pause to reflect and listen.

December 24

Joy to the World

*"But the angel said to them, 'Do not be afraid. I bring you good news that will cause great joy for all the people. Today in the town of David a Savior has been born to you; he is the Messiah, the Lord.'" **Luke 2:10-11***

DEVOTIONAL

Joy isn't found in perfect circumstances but in the blessings that surround us every day, inviting us to pause and appreciate the love woven into our lives.

DAILY REFLECTION

What brings you true joy in your life right now, and how can you share that joy with others? Consider the blessings and love surrounding you, and think about how they can be amplified in your world.

PRAYER

Dear Lord, thank you for the joy that fills our hearts, even in the midst of life's challenges. Help us to recognize and spread that joy to those around us, so that we may reflect your love in our lives.

Joy is not just a feeling; it's a gift we share with the world.

December 25

Peace Beyond the Presents

"Peace I leave with you; my peace I give you. I do not give to you as the world gives. Do not let your hearts be troubled and do not be afraid."
John 14:27

DEVOTIONAL

Letting go of the pressure to create a perfect holiday allows us to embrace the joy in our hearts and the relationships that matter most.

DAILY REFLECTION

What does it mean to you to have peace amid the busyness and chaos of everyday life? How can you invite that peace into your heart today?

PRAYER

Dear God, thank You for the gift of peace that surpasses all understanding. Help us to find calm in the present moment, trusting in Your loving presence as we navigate our daily challenges.

True peace often blossoms in the quiet spaces between our busy schedules.

December 26

Looking Back with Gratitude

"Enter his gates with thanksgiving and his courts with praise; give thanks to him and praise his name." **Psalm 100:4**

DEVOTIONAL

Embrace your past with a heart full of gratitude, for it has woven the beautiful tapestry of who you are today.

DAILY REFLECTION

What moments from the past year are you most grateful for, and how have they shaped the woman and mother you are today?

PRAYER

Dear God, thank You for the journey thus far. Help me to embrace the lessons of the past with a heart full of gratitude, knowing they have brought me closer to You.

Gratitude turns what we have into enough.

December 27

Preparing for the New

"For I know the plans I have for you, declares the LORD, plans to prosper you and not to harm you, plans to give you hope and a future."
Jeremiah 29:11

DEVOTIONAL

Every season holds a promise; take a moment to breathe and trust that something beautiful is on the horizon for you.

DAILY REFLECTION

What new beginnings are you sensing God might be calling you to in this season of your life? How can you prepare your heart and mind to embrace these changes with faith?

PRAYER

Dear God, thank You for the promise of new beginnings. As I step into this new season, help me to trust in Your guidance and embrace the journey ahead with an open heart.

Every ending is a new beginning waiting to unfold; trust the process.

December 28

He's Already in Tomorrow

"I will instruct you and teach you in the way you should go; I will counsel you with my loving eye on you." **Psalm 32:8**

DEVOTIONAL

No matter what you're facing today, remember that God's presence extends into your tomorrows, providing comfort and guidance in every season of life.

DAILY REFLECTION

What concerns or worries about tomorrow can you hand over to God today, trusting that He's already in your future?

PRAYER

Dear God, thank you for being in every moment of our lives. Help me to release my worries about tomorrow and embrace the peace that comes from knowing You are already there.

Tomorrow's burdens are not ours to bear today;
let us rest in the knowledge that God is already paving the way.

December 29

Finishing the Year in Faith

"Now faith is confidence in what we hope for and assurance about what we do not see." **Hebrews 11:1**

DEVOTIONAL

Our faith often grows in the in-between moments—those times when we are simply learning to embrace the uncertainties of life with grace and hope.

DAILY REFLECTION

What challenges or blessings have defined your year so far, and how can you see God's hand in each moment as you navigate the final days ahead?

PRAYER

Dear Lord, thank You for walking with us throughout this year. As we prepare to close this chapter, help us to embrace the lessons learned and the faith that has grown within us. May we trust in Your plans for our future.

Faith isn't just about believing: it's about knowing that every step. even the hardest ones. leads us closer to Him.

December 30

God's Faithfulness Never Ends

"Though the mountains be shaken and the hills be removed, yet my unfailing love for you will not be shaken, nor my covenant of peace be removed," says the Lord, who has compassion on you. **Isaiah 54:10**

DEVOTIONAL

God's faithfulness is a constant reminder that even in our most chaotic days, we are never alone; He walks beside us every step of the way.

DAILY REFLECTION

What moments in your life have you witnessed God's unwavering faithfulness, even amidst challenges and doubts? How can remembering these moments shape your current circumstances?

PRAYER

Dear Lord, thank you for your constant presence in my life. Help me to recognize and celebrate your faithfulness each day, reminding me that I am never alone in my journey.

God's love is the anchor that holds us steady in life's storms.

December 31

Grace to End the Year Well

"Let us then approach God's throne of grace with confidence, so that we may receive mercy and find grace to help us in our time of need." **Hebrews 4:16**

DEVOTIONAL

In the hustle of life, remember that grace allows us to embrace the present with hope and assurance, empowering us to end the year well.

DAILY REFLECTION

What does it look like for you to extend grace to yourself as this year comes to a close? How can you let go of the pressures you've placed on yourself and embrace the journey of the past months?

PRAYER

Dear God, as I approach the end of this year, help me to see the moments of grace You've bestowed upon me. May my heart be filled with gratitude and hope for all that is to come, trusting in Your perfect plan.

Grace invites us to pause, reflect, and embrace both our triumphs and trials with a heart full of love.

More Devotionals from Anchored Grace

If this devotional encouraged your heart, you may also enjoy these devotionals from Anchored Grace.

- 365 Day Devotional for Women
- 90 Day Devotional for Women Seeking Peace
- 90 Day Devotional for Women Facing Anxiety and Stress
- 90 Day Devotional for Women 50+
- Guided Prayer Journal for Women

Search **"Anchored Grace Devotional"** on Amazon to discover more devotionals designed to support your journey of faith.

Thank You
for Walking This Journey

Thank you for spending this devotional journey with Anchored Grace.

If this devotional encouraged your heart, strengthened your faith, or brought peace to your daily routine, would you consider leaving a short review on Amazon?

devo.anchoredgraces.com/2026

Reviews help other women discover devotionals that may support them through their own seasons of life.

Even a single sentence about your experience can make a difference.

We are grateful you chose Anchored Grace.